SOLIDIFYING THE RELATIONSHIP BETWEEN THE PASTOR AND ASSOCIATE MINISTERS

Copyright © 2016 Rosetta Lee-Epps Skates
All rights reserved.

CONTENTS

ACKNOWLEDGEMENTS — iv

DEDICATION — v

EPIGRAPH — vi

INTRODUCTION — 1

CHAPTER ONE: MINISTRY FOCUS — 8

CHAPTER TWO: BIBLICAL FOUNDATIONS — 37

CHAPTER THREE: THEOLOGICAL FOUNDATIONS — 70

CHAPTER FOUR: PROJECT ANALYSIS — 82

APPENDIX A: QUESTIONNAIRE / SURVEY — 102

APPENDIX B: PRE AND POST TEST QUESTIONNAIRE — 105

APPENDIX C: ASSOCIATE MINISTER'S TRAINING CLASS — 107

APPENDIX D: SAMPLE CODE OF ETHICS — 109

BIBLIOGRAPHY — 116

ACKNOWLEDGEMENTS

I would like to thank my family and friends for their support and patience in this process. I would also like to express gratitude to my mentors Dr. Terry Thomas, Dr. Reginald Dawkins for their guidance, support, encouragement, feedback, and instructions over the course of this Doctor of Ministry program. In addition, I would also like to acknowledge the contributions of my professional associates, Dr. Michael C. Turner, Dr. Howard Willis, Jr., and Dr. Elmore E. Warren, Jr.

I also owe a debt of gratitude to my editors, Dr. Jeremiah Hackley, Dr. Lori D. Spears, Dr. Candy R. Hardy for their support and work throughout the project. Also, a special thanks to my context associates and peers for blessing me with their support. I am grateful to Geraline Boggs for her endurance.

Finally, I want to acknowledge and thank the Dean for Doctoral Studies, Dr. Harold Hudson, and Administrative Assistant, Janice Kronour for their consistent encouragement and aiding me to complete this endeavor in ministry.

DEDICATION

This work is dedicated to my grandmother and my mother who gave me guidance and created the hunger in me for the knowledge of God. In addition, this work is dedicated to my husband Glenn, family and friends that have been on this journey with me for the past three years. A special dedication is given to my church for the support and encouragement, especially my pastor and the associate ministers. I thank all persons I met along the way and thank God for my life.

I can do all this through him who gives me strength.
Philippians 4:13 NIV

INTRODUCTION

The purpose and intent of this writing is to create a project that will help to motivate Associate Ministers to consider their positions in a higher regard. The morale has been somewhat low, so this project will define positions and hopefully motivate the Associate Ministers to do their best. The Associate Minister is assigned the Pastor to head an assigned ministry as the President. The Associate Minister should see him or herself as a leader in control of a ministry. Secondly, the Associate Minister should support the Pastor. Also, the Associate Minister should be a servant/helper to the congregation.

The problem that has been encountered or seen by the Special Assistant to the Pastor is that the Associate Ministers are not motivated to rise to the high level of excellency in doing the assigned church ministry. The Pastor is aware that the Associate minister is capable of handling the assignment, however, the Associate Minister is lacking in realizing what the expected duties are. The solidifying of the relationship between the Pastor and Associate Ministers should result in the Associate Ministers performing to a high level. The hypothesis for this project is that if training is provided the pastor and associate ministers will have a better relationship. The training should create more concern for service than preaching.

This project seeks to find ways or steps that can be taken to explain to Associate Ministers that are called to preach that there is more to being an Associate Minister than preaching. The project will examine case studies, do interviews, and use a question survey to find ways and steps to motivate the Associate Minister to get beyond the desire to preach and perform other duties that will be for the good and welfare of the church. The problem facing The Miracle Center of Faith Missionary Baptist Church at Capitol Heights, Maryland is defined as a low level of motivation by Associate Ministers which is a concern for the context church. The solidifying of the relationship between the Pastor and Associate Ministers will bring about a better understanding.

There are some Associate Ministers that fail to advance to a high level of excellence while serving as Associate Ministers.

Further, the purpose of this Project Proposal is to have ongoing research to find new ways to develop new skills or new approaches to raise the levels of excellence. Also, to find ways to solve problems that has created the low levels of excellence for the Associate Ministers. Also, as the project is researched, what can motivate the Associate Minister to support the Pastor and help the Congregation, while maintaining a high level of motivation for oneself? Possibly, the self-interest and passion for the Church Ministry assignment will be the basis for creating the steps to keep the Associate Ministers motivated. Since, every knee will bow and every tongue will confess Jesus Christ, it is a good thing for Associate Ministers to be motivated to the highest level possible through serving the Pastor and congregation. All in the Church should conduct themselves as servants of Jesus Christ and the Associate Ministers can lead the way to serve.

At this time, a survey has been prepared. The survey is in work, reviewed, and continuing to receive input and questions that lead to farther research. The Associate Ministers are shocked that such a Study and research is being done that involves the observation of them and require responses from them. It appears that when persons know they are part of a study, attitudes improve, questions and concerns arise. This is a positive reaction, however, it can also, be a negative reaction. Appendix A will give details of the first questionnaire, survey. This questionnaire, survey has begun the physical output that will require input from the Associate Ministers. Second, it will be shown that Case Studies will provide meaningful answers for questions about motivation and answers to how to deal with motivation for the Associate Ministers. More research and input will take place to gather steps that can be used by The Miracle Center of Faith Missionary Baptist Church.

Also, the steps can or will be used by any other church or organization that require support from followers. Followers should realize that they are also, leaders, but in a role that has a higher Leader.

The Associate Ministers Survey suggests that the ability of the Associate Ministers can be based on their response to each question. The desired result was to find the self-interest and passion of each Associate Minister for service and support to the Pastor and congregation. Based on the overall results, it is apparent that there is a low level of motivation that needs to be addressed. For example, one Associate Minister expressed a desire to work in Prison Ministry. However, the person did not follow through to take the necessary training. When training was done by others, the reaction was, "it's My Ministry." In conclusion, it may be their self-interest or passion, but if the person does not follow through on the assignment, then the leader is a failure. Further, is it fair to stand just as tall, waiting for a preaching assignment? The question becomes obvious to the Pastor; can the person be counted on for service?

In support of the Questionnaire, Survey, research has been done through the reading of books that express the reactions of called Ministers. When Ministers are assigned to certain ministries of the Church, some will accept the challenge and excel in the position. For example, the Homeless Ministry has become the strongest ministry of the Church. The person assigned had self-interest and a passion for the Ministry and position of Leader. Each month, The Miracle Center of Faith Missionary Baptist Church does make 300 sandwiches with snack treats and water to be distributed in the Maryland and Washington, D.C. area to selected locations. To this day, the Church vehicle is known throughout Maryland and Washington D.C. for the service to the Homeless. However, there is such a phrase, "do not get weary in well doing." A few months ago, the Leader, Associate Minister, became weary in the position and stepped down from the Leadership role. It was maintained that health drove the Associate Minister to make this decision. However, it is the opinion, in support of this Project Proposal that the Associate Minister had the option of remaining as the Leader of Homeless Ministry and uses the empowerment given by the Pastor to assign others to carry out certain duties and just oversee.

If one is alive and well, it is the duty of the Associate Minister to delegate the work assignment to an able bodied person. However, the Associate Minister continued to try to do the harder work and was not able to perform. This is a time when a person will become weary. When a person becomes weary, their faith and endurance becomes challenged. When this situation occurs, usually, a person will quit, complain, or begin to just not show up for the assignment. From this case study, it was determined that the lead Associate Minister, became "weary in well doing" and gave up on the empowered position. The Pastor at the context location, The Miracle Center of Faith Missionary Baptist Church is a man of action. When there is a situation to address, he takes action in a sure and quick manner that keeps a position of situation running smooth without many questions. His leadership ability has bought much comfort to the members. As a Doctor of Ministry, he is very much aware of the requirements that are necessary to lead a Church and can maintain harmony in the community, and up to the State, and World level. He had demonstrated that with regard to theory and practice, he knows that Christ is in the midst of all foundation requirements, i.e. Biblical, Historical, Theological, and Theoretical. He is aware that each foundation will show concepts, methods, and confirm the Gospel, Good News of Jesus Christ.

Through the context of The Miracle Center of Faith Missionary Baptist Church the gospel is based on the Baptist religion to build the foundation of the Apostles and Prophets. Matthew 16:13-20 let's one know that Jesus asked his Disciples, "Whom do men say that I am?" Then Peter, answering said, "Thou are the loving Christ, son of the living God..." The Miracle Center of Faith Missionary Baptist Church embraces this Theological foundation as the basis for serving God and integrating all of the Christian theology. Even further, is the embracing of the Holy Ghost on the day of Pentecost. Through the Pastor, the theological foundation of The Miracle Center of Faith Missionary Baptist Church has grown over the past twenty three years by a beginning Mission Statement, along with... and the establishing of Ministries to support the Pastor and Congregation. The Pastor is known for his theoretical knowledge. He develops thoughts, hears from God through visions, and is often found to grow with an action plan to set out plans according to what "Thus saith the Lord." He is a firm believer in hearing from the Lord and establishing a plan on solid ground. The Researcher cannot think of any failure in the Pastor. However, the Congregation has failed to live up to some of his expectations. When those situations occur, he is careful to have a work around plan and continues to move forward. The Pastor is known to be an encourager. He will help any person find or see potential in him or herself. Many testimonies are told during events, i.e., upcoming 23rd Anniversary, the past Family and Friends Day, and upcoming 40th Anniversary, June 9, 2014 will be times of testimonies. These are times when one can find out about the Theological foundations that have been set at The Miracle Center of Faith Missionary Baptist Church. The steps that will be taken to bring the Associate Ministers to the level of his expectations will help guide other Pastors to the same satisfaction that will come soon to The Miracle Center of Faith Missionary Baptist Church. As it has happen before, other Pastor will say to this Pastor, "we are going to follow your example." The Pastor is a practical person. However, he can be found looking at theoretical, but careful to relate to the theological, to be sure that God is in his thoughts. The Biblical base is always apparent at The Miracle Center of Faith Missionary Baptist Church. The Researcher is known to quote 1Timothy 2:7, "Consider what I say and the Lord give thee understanding in all things." Also, the Pastor can be found preaching and literally standing on the actual Bible for demonstration purposes. In times like these, I will recall Dr. Miles J. Jones, for his expression of, "Preaching is an Art, Paint the Picture"[1] The questionnaire/survey was titled, The Associate Minister. See Appendix A.

Research Methods

---

[1]Miles J. Jones, Dr., *Classroom time*, April 4, 2004 (Richmond, VA: Virginia Union University), 2004.

The pre-test methodology of the survey utilized ten questions or statements regarding the associate ministers feeling about church ministry. This pre-test was administered during the eight week project assignment. Following the training and teaching by the pastor. The post-test was a repeated version of the pre-test in an effort to find out if after seven weeks of training and teaching if the associate ministers attitudes would be changed. By solidifying the relationship between the pastor and the associate ministers it should be a better understanding of duties.

Chapter One defines the ministry focus by examining the synergy between my context and me. This chapter explains my spiritual beginning, examines the context of the project and concludes with a discussion about how my spiritual process has come to the need for pastors to find ways to receive support as well as service from the associate ministers. This chapter examines this synergy and brings forth the design and testing of the model of ministry after the problem has been presented.

Chapter Two presents the biblical foundation for this ministry using selected passages from both the Old Testament and New Testament. For each passage, the foundation discusses how the details in each passage support the design of the model of ministry. An examination of each of these texts present much information as to what a pastor can do by solidifying the relationship between him and associate ministers. This foundation begins with the Old Testament text by explaining how Miriam and Aaron became discouraged when their brother, Moses, married an Ethiopian woman. They questioned whether God had only spoken to Moses. This was not a good situation, because the Lord heard them and was not pleased. It was noted in Numbers, chapter twelve, verse three, that Moses was very meek, above all men in the world. At this point, the Lord called Moses, Aaron and Miriam to the tabernacle for a meeting. Then, the Lord came down to the tabernacle in a pillar of the cloud and stood in the door of the tabernacle. He spoke to them, mainly Aaron and Miriam. The Lord told them if a prophet was among them, he would make himself know through a vision and in a dream. However, he let them know that Moses was faithful and he would speak to him mouth to mouth. The Lord questioned Aaron and Miriam why they were not afraid to speak against Moses. Therefore, the Lord became angry and departed away from them. However, as the Lord departed, Miriam became leprous, white as snow. When Aaron show that Miriam was leprous, he asked Moses to forgive them for their sin, because they were foolish. Then Moses cried unto the Lord to heal his sister, Miriam. The Lord punished Miriam with leprosy for seven days, to remain outside the camp.

The New Testament continues the awareness of leadership through Jesus. When Jesus washed the Disciples feet, he demonstrated that as a Master, he could still serve. Primarily, John 13:14, "If I then, your Lord and Master, have washed your feet, ye also ought to wash one another's feet." The New Testament foundation presents John 13:14 wherein Jesus places a towel around his waist and began to wash the feet of the disciples. Through this gesture, Jesus allows the disciples a chance to that he was the master, yet he was able to wash their feet. This foundation gave the disciples a lesson about being a leader as well as a servant.

Chapter Three discusses a theological foundation for the model of ministry and use liberation theology for this purpose. The Theological Foundation for the course or focus is on Preaching and Leadership in the Black Church. Based on the proposed project dealing with the motivation of the Associate Ministers, the Theological Foundation will be a benefit to those interested in religion in support of the Pastor.

Chapter Four, the project analysis, examines the effort to explore the processes necessary for solidifying the relationship of the Pastor and Associate Ministers in a model of ministry in order to arrive at a hypothesis for what is necessary to produce this model in the context church. The thesis is the following: Solidifying the relationship of the Pastor and Associate Ministers is dependent upon engaging them in church ministry that addresses their self- interest and passion.

CHAPTER ONE

MINISTRY FOCUS

The purpose of writing this paper is to provide points of synergy on my life events, passion, and focus for the proposed research. I will discuss the following: (1) synergy, (2) pivotal/vital or critical points in my life journey, (3) passion as an outgrowth of major life events, (4) the called purpose and (5) the proposed research focus. Six, (6), expound on the needs that are in the context, (7), the skills that are brought to the ministry context and (8), how the needs and skills meet in the proposed project. Through this Doctor of Ministry project I will attempt to write guidelines that can be used to motivate leaders for greatness. This greatness is based on the Associate Minister choosing a church ministry to satisfy his or her self- interest and passion. When successful, becoming known, in the chosen church ministry, the greatness will build as a process.

My life journey had events that occurred to create impacts that will last a lifetime. I have a passion for love. I believe that love can cure almost anything. My favorite expression is, "all about love." Knowing that God is love has made a major difference in my life. As far back as I can remember my mother told her that life is not perfect. By knowing that life is not perfect, I am able to glamorize, almost any situation. I was born in the era of fairy tales, stories with happy endings, Shakespeare, religious values, moral values and Dr. Martin Luther King Jr.'s peace and love speeches. I believe that people should be trustworthy and love one another. I believe in love, marriage, and happy ever after. However, my life has not fallen this way. Despite, my ups and downs, I can be found saying, "count it all joy."[1] Perhaps, the way life went early during my Federal Government career is the

---

[1]The Holy Bible, New International Version: James 1:2 Unless otherwise noted, all scripture references in this document are from the NIV.

reason why I had a need to investigate the issue of Associate Ministers. I have dealt with groups of persons that only want to do the one assigned duty. However, one should realize there are other duties that need attention. In the context church, The Miracle Center of Faith Missionary Baptist Church the Associate Ministers only want to preach. However, there are more assignments that are required to be done. I moved around in the Prince George's County area of Maryland, to various churches where I discovered that other churches had similar situations.

As I look back over my life, I realize that my mother's life had an impact on me. My mother would be eighty six years old now, if she were alive. However, she passed away, December 11, 2005. I have many memories of things my mother and I talked about. Of major importance is the fact that my mother conceived a child before she was married. This event in her life overwhelmed my life, because my mother and I grew to be best friends. The term overwhelming effects reflect in my life to the present day. I was constantly aware of what happened to my mother and wanted to prevent the repeat of history through me. Being a helper became my passion. I have become that person that a supervisor or pastor could rely on. I still enjoy children and spend my retired time as a Substitute Teacher. I spend time helping children at church through Sunday School classes, Women's Ministry, Youth Council meetings and other social events.

Persons should have plans for their lives. Many persons will think of what they would like to do. This is good, but writing the plan is better. Information that is written is the best method. unwritten, oral information has to be recalled. History will inform us that the Afro-Americans culture told many stories. These stories were told, but not recorded. Therefore, someone else could take the oral story and document it as if they wrote it and claim it as their own. It is sad to think of life experiences that could have been used as history, but were not written. More than likely, someone has already wrote steps or plans that could have been used by the pastor to document duties for the associate ministers. One has to be careful about claiming the information that was provided to persons in a church. There are times when the information is passed along from one person to another without any documentation. It is taken for granted that all is well and trust in what is said. Then when the information needs to be recalled it is from memory, which can be limited. Also, some persons use the fact that information was not documented to make excuses for whatever he or she has not accomplished.

My proposed research is based on Preaching and Leadership in the Black Church. Since I am a preacher, I have concerns about being a better preacher. Also, as a past Executive Minister and returning Associate Minister, my concern is how to support my pastor at an excellent or high level. The high or excellent level is based on text from the Ministerial Ethics stating,

I will be supportive and loyal to the senior pastor or, if unable to do so, will seek another place of service. I will be supportive and loyal to my fellow staff ministers, never criticizing them or undermining their ministry. I will recognize my role and responsibility on the church staff and will not feel threatened or in competition with other ministers of my special area of ministry. Lastly, if single, I will be discreet in my dating practices, especially in relation to members of my congregation.[2]

I am presently, Special Assistant to the Pastor and for over four years have been the President of the Minister's Council. At this time, I am concerned about the Associate Ministers. My proposed research is on solidifying the relationship between the Pastor and Associate Ministers by establishing boundaries and levels of performance expectation. In solidifying the relationship, the end result is motivation of the Associate Ministers to rise to an excellent level of support to the pastor.

The Miracle Center of Faith Missionary Baptist Church has many leaders. However, there is a need for more Associate Ministers to desire to want to support the Pastor. The Pastor, Rev. Dr. MCT, Sr., is intentional about discovering the passion and identifying Spiritual

---

[2] Joe E. Trull and James E. Carter, *Ministerial Ethics: Moral Formation for Church Leaders* (Grand Rapids, MI: Baker Academic, 2004), 262.

Gifts of the Associate Minister. However, he cannot always determine who will be present for the training. If people miss the scheduled training, what should be done to make up for the training? Further, I had previously served as Executive Minister/Pastor at a planted church in LaPlata, Maryland during the years of 2010-2011. Presently, as a Special Assistant to the Pastor and leading Amour Bearer, I am expected to be a leader striving for excellence continually.

The Associate Ministers are expected to primarily support the pastor in carrying out the mandates and policies set for by the larger church. He or she is expected to be faithful, committed, and consistent. There have been persons who feel they should have certain positions, but have not been faithful, committed and consistent in maintaining a level of good work. As a support to the pastor they serve as amour bearers, chairperson/leader of ministries, such as Sick Ministry, Prison Ministry, Homeless Ministry, Consoling Ministry, Pastoral Care and Counseling Ministry, Sharing Ministry, Missionary Ministry, Evangelism Ministry, etc. Further, I am the Chairperson for the Job Placement Ministry. Also, I am the Chairperson for Education for the Social Action Ministry. This ministry falls under the heading of Partnership for the Renewal in Southern and Central Maryland, (PRISCM). PRISCM is a Social Action Ministry in and for the community, which has been discussed in the Spiritual Journey documentation. I am busy and want to help other Associate Ministers be busy doing work for God. How can the Associate Ministers be motivated to do work in the church to a level of excellence? As I do my research project it will be interesting to follow what pattern will lead to why I am so motivated. Also, in doing research for the project, it will be interesting to see what will come forward to motivate others.

There will be questions about whether a leader should be chosen or come forward and ask to be a leader. For example, As Amour Bearers, the Associate Ministers move around with the Pastor and First Lady to ensure that all areas are safe and people around them serve in their best interest. The amour bearer provides and maintains a positive atmosphere in the services. They are in place to be responsible for any situation that may arise. They are under the authority of the Pastor. They receive further guidance from the Assistant to the Pastor, the Special Assistant to the Pastor, and the President of the Minister's Council. They should uphold the excellent serve standards of ministry and be leaders in the church. Each Associate Minister should preach and communicate spiritually with the congregation when required. The Pastor has informed me and others, "when you see the need, do it!" It is a priority to take care of the needs of the people, immediately. Being a compassionate person is a must. The Associate Minister must know how to communicate and help all persons, from babies to seniors.

The Associate Ministers should have (1) an open heart to serve, (2) open heart to stand on the word of God and (3) an open heart to speak about the word of God. Many of the Associate Ministers have not been attending the Minister's workshops, training sessions, and sharing sessions that have been scheduled. When their turn to serve as lead for Holy Communion or Baptism, or preach for a funeral at the community funeral home, they are not prepared. There are times when one will panic if a friend wants him or her to perform/officiate for a wedding. These are learned skills that are taught by the pastor. However, the Associate Ministers have not attended the scheduled training. What can one do to motivate the Associate Ministers? "Leadership is the art of motivating a group of people to act towards achieving a common goal.[3]" There are persons that appear to have leadership abilities that come natural to them. However, most of the time leadership is a learned ability.

The need to motivate leaders in The Miracle Center of Faith Missionary Baptist Church has been examined in the Context Analysis. The primary focused project rest with the Associate Ministers to narrow the focus of the proposed project. However, the motivation techniques that will be presented in the research project can be used by all leaders. The basis of the project is solidifying the relationship between the Pastor and Associate Ministers. In doing so, this will show ways to motivate the Associate Ministers to be in place

---

[3]Susan Ward, Access dated May 2015, www.ask.com (Canada), 2015.

to support the Pastor. The general nature of this project is to motivate the Associate Minister and let them know that their work and effort are not in vain. The work and efforts will make one ready to step into the pastor's position if needed or required. However, it is definitely necessary that one should know not to wait on the pastor's position, but to become skilled and available to fill other Church openings, other inside positions or be prepared to fill vacancies in other churches. There are networks, such as the Clergy Caucus, Minister's Council and American Baptist Churches of the South (ABCOTS) that the Pastors of many churches are part of and know when other churches have a need for assistance.

In conclusion, how this proposed project will be approached through a research setting will be challenging. With the skills that I possess in ministry, good success is expected. Through this Doctor of Ministry project there will be research and steps to take to fulfill the requirements.

Spiritual Autobiography

I was born to two generations of spiritual heritage from my father and mother. My father, mother, and grandparents were spiritual persons who passed on a Godly legacy. The unwritten stories of religious beliefs and how they tried to live can be passed on to the family. Each person is deceased, but thoughts and memories linger on in my heart.

Early memories of my maternal grandmother include quoting scriptures, encouraging the young children and the other grandchildren to live according to how they were taught, shaped my spiritual legacy. This grandmother would say that the road to hell will be crowded, but the road to heaven would be few. She taught us to stay on the road to heaven. Due to the strong influences of this grandmother and her contemporaries, spiritual growth was not just a matter of personal faith, but also family heritage. I attempt to live to please God. I am grateful that God let me have a grandmother, father and mother as examples of righteousness and faith before my eyes.

I spent time talking with my mother about the past years. Through these conversations I learned about my life from birth to four years old. The words that were spoken from my mother about the years before the age of four are only memories. I was encouraged by my mother to learn to cook, sew, shop, and be a little mother, before the age of six years old. I believe that my spirit followed the lineage of my grandmother and mother for a spiritual foundation.

My grandmother and mother were strong spiritual women. I believe they should have been preachers. The calling to ministry has been a joy for me. My spiritual journey has been a walk by faith. I have experienced some good and bad times. Perhaps, being country born and knowing that life is not perfect has made me accept life as it comes. I have known of God since I was four years old. As one reads my spiritual journey, it will reveal some experiences that show how God has molded me. Also, having a career with the Central

Intelligence Agency has made me careful about revealing secrets from the past.

The spiritual family heritage is influenced by my father. He was born in Farmville, Virginia, the son of a farmer. By the grace of God, Grandfather came out of slavery and acquired over seventy acres of land. He lived a spiritual life while raising horses, cattle, pigs, chickens and other animals. He was an entrepreneur who walked by faith. God blessed him with knowledge for the growing and selling of tobacco, sugar cane, wheat and corn. His way of life provided for his family.

My brothers and sisters visited the farm during the summer. I often heard him conducting business with buyers. I noticed that the buyers called him "Captain". I once made the comment to my brothers, "All the white men are named Captain." My paternal grandmother worked in the homes of the whites in the Virginia area until she became sick and passed away.

My maternal grandmother was born in the Appomattox, Virginia area and relocated to Farmville, Virginia. She was married to my grandfather. My father and mother did not know each other in Farmville, Virginia. They both relocated to Baltimore, Maryland and there met each other. They were married in 1945. During this time, my maternal grandfather heard through his friends about the coal mines in West Virginia. He moved his family to Fayette County, West Virginia. Later, my mother and father traveled to West Virginia. My grandfather introduced my father to the coal mines. My parents began a new life in West Virginia.

I was told by my mother that life in West Virginia was different from living in Baltimore. My mother became pregnant with her first child from her new husband. However, she had a child from a previous relationship. She was the first born child from the other relationship that my mother referred to as date rape. My mother was on a double date with a friend, but she did not care for the person chosen for her. However, she was caught in a situation that resulted in a child being born. I am the fourth child of my mother and the first daughter of my father. Therefore, I have two older brothers and one older sister.

I was born in Kincaid, West Virginia in a small coal mining community. I am proud of the fact that I am a black coal miner's daughter and will not hesitate to let you know that. I will declare, "I am like Loretta Lynn, a coal miner's daughter."[4] However, the reason for this in-depth story about my humble beginnings is because of the history of the kind of people I have encountered. People can be cruel, even some Christians. Some don't even want to believe that there are black people from West Virginia. I have received degrading letters about West Virginia. The cruel ones may be born in small areas of Virginia or Pennsylvania, but believe they are better than those born in West Virginia.

Also, there are those born in Charleston or Beckley, West Virginia who believe they are better than those born in or near the coal mining areas. It is a form of cruelty to be put down about your community. All my life, I have lived with this stigma. I am ready to help others deal with situations that affect their self- image. I learned my style from TV and wore hand me downs I received from the rich white women that were wives to the car dealers. My father worked for a car dealership after retiring from the coal mining company.

Thinking back, at the age of four years old, I was aware that my mother enjoyed going to church. I realize that getting to know Jesus is the best thing I have ever done. Through my knowledge of Jesus, I have learned that even His family and others did not respect Him properly. The Scriptures inform us that some people remarked, "Can anything good come out of Nazareth?"[5] as well as, "Is not this the carpenter's son?" [6]

I have helped persons on my Federal government job. Also, I can be found at the Miracle Center of Faith Missionary Baptist Church helping someone with a life issue. I have been known to have women fall at my feet in church asking how to deal with marriage situations. I am blessed by God with a calm personality that allows me to gather

---

[4]Ask.com., Loretta Lynn, Access dated February 17, 2013.biography.com
[5] John 1:46, NIV
[6]Matthew 13:55, NIV

the needed information before giving advice. During the snow storm of 2000, I lay in bed with the Holy Bible beside me and studied the life of King David. This makes me strong in my belief that God is a forgiving God. This keeps me forgiving persons, even when I feel that I am treated unfairly. I will find a way to try to resolve an issue with a peaceful outcome. My all about love attitude has made my path in life one that does have detours. I will back away from certain conflicts and seek a way that all involved can feel like a winner.

For me, life is about seeing the joy in life and keeping joy in my spirit. I keep the phrase "count it all joy" taken from James 1:2 in my heart. I could have had many pity parties and would have invited people. For example, I could tell about a date that went wrong. I was slapped and I jumped from the car. I could tell of the parties where many types of drugs were offered, but I refused them. I learned to drink orange juice, ginger ale and Pepsi, but still party like the others that were drinking hard liquor and using drugs. My father had warned me that a woman should never let herself get drunk, because men would take advantage of her. My mother always told me that no one has a perfect life; therefore, she accepted life as it came. I am mindful of my blessings and keep myself moving forward.

During my birthday month of October, I enjoy reflecting back over my past experiences to see how far God has brought me. I realize that through the grace and mercy of Jesus I am still alive. When I think of how Jesus was treated in spite of his goodness, it still gives me pain. Knowing that people will still treat me wrong despite my own goodness cause me to continue to keep a shield around my heart. You will often hear me say, "It's all about love," even though I am protecting my heart from pain.

Love is important to me. I was always curious about what love really meant. For me love needs to be defined and I want to see the actions of love. There are times when a person will say that they love you, but really do not show a caring way to express the love. I expect the showing of love to be in the form of kindness.

At age six, I learned that my mother had asthma and at this point, my life changed due to her mother's illness. I had to learn how to shop, cook, clean, serve and take care of my brothers and sisters. Whenever my mother was sick, those chores fell on me much harder. I became much more aware of life as my mother became pregnant again and again. The house was becoming crowded with children. There were more mouths to feed, more dishes to wash, more clothes to be washed and yet, school homework had to be done. I began to dread the recurring experiences. Eventually, my mother was too sick to continue to have children, but my father would not consider the use of birth control.

As I grew, from age six to twelve years old, I became more and more curious about what was going on around me. I listened to some of the discussions between my parents. In my opinion, my father was not showing enough emotional love and support to such a sick wife. The doctors recommended birth control to stop having children after the seventh child, but my father refused. My mother was so ill at times that I did not believe that she would live to see me grow up. At this point, I began to be disappointed with my father. I believed that my father and mother should find a method to stop having so many children. Why was his love for me fading? I thought it was because there were so many children to love. Why was his love for my mother fading? My father was not as compassionate as I believed he should be. When my mother had asthma attacks, he complained and was not helpful. Then, why was my love fading for my father?

From age four to eleven, I believed I was such a happy child. I was called, little mother and my mother had also, become my friend. By age twelve, I began to notice more changes from my father. There were more brothers and sisters that made the house full of children. At age thirteen, I really felt unloved by my father. He would not let me go out of the house with my brothers anymore. There were more rules and beatings when they disobeyed. My father kept saying, stay away from the neighborhood boys. He would say, kissing leads to something. He never told me what it led to, but he was so harsh about whatever it was. I became afraid that my mother might pass away. In fact, my mother did leave home, but returned to save me. She knew that I would be stuck with all the children. I had prayed to God when I became afraid. At this point, God was good to me and sustained my mother. My mother continued to have children.

At age thirteen, I was baptized at the Ingram Grove Baptist Church in West Virginia. I began to sing in the choir. Later, I began to teach Sunday school to the younger youths. Sunday school lessons were important to me and I kept records of all the classes that I had attended and those that I taught. Some of the lessons helped me learn that God has unconditional love for people. This love included me and I am always aware of his love. Therefore, I have a desire to give back to others. Still in the back of my mind, thoughts lingered. I told my mother that I did not want a house full of children like she had, nor did I want a mean man like my father. I had decided when I became grown, I would treat myself as an only child. I did not know what the future would hold, but I did believe in love. This belief in love would give me hope for the future.

At age seventeen, I had seven brothers and four sisters. This same year my mother was pregnant again, but did not know that she was having a child. I noticed Mom's stomach getting larger again and asked my mother if she were having another child. My mother replied, no. However, a few months later, she suffered a miscarriage. After this miscarriage, my mother was physically unable to bear any more children. Perhaps, at this time, I thought even more seriously, that I did not want many children.

Growing up in church, from age four to seventeen years old, I would watch the pastor, deacons, choir members and others very closely. I liked church. However, I remember, one time at approximately four years old, I kicked the back of one of the pews. The deacon touched my legs to stop me. I never forgot the authority that he showed in that moment. I knew the deacon was the second leader following the pastor. I do not remember ever breaking another rule at church. The deacon was the Sunday school teacher. Another deacon was very strict, but I still liked the classes. There were some boys that were mischievous in the class settings. The deacon would let them know that they were causing trouble for themselves. He told them their time for living could be limited for doing wrong. I paid attention in class and prayed to please God. I often prayed for the health of my mother and was grateful for all that God had done for her. I knew that I would always be grateful and do something to let God know.

As a young teenager, approximately, sixteen years old, I sat on the railroad tracks, prayed, and asked God to show me the world. I was becoming disappointed with the strict rules and the taking care of babies. I was curious about love and felt that my father had lost the compassion that I saw in him as a little girl. My mother continued to hold on to their marriage. She assured me that there was a life for me in the world. I asked God to let me look beyond the trees and mountains. I wanted to experience some of the things that I saw on TV. God answered my prayer, one day, during an English class. At that time, I was in the eleventh grade. A recruiter from the Central Intelligence Agency office in Charleston, West Virginia came to Collins High School in Oak Hill, West Virginia. The Recruiter asked the class if anyone would like to work in Washington, D.C. I raised my hand immediately. One year later, upon completion of High School, I was on my way to Washington, D.C. to work for the government. I had two older brothers that had already relocated to the city. They lived with a paternal aunt and a maternal uncle. My aunt owned a row house where my two brothers, my uncle and I rented rooms from her. I found the city exciting. The bright lights, the music of the African American culture and meeting so many people enthralled me. It was great. I enjoyed seeing Afro-Americans, my people, doing so many different jobs. Being able to move around from place to place, whenever I pleased was great for me.

I began working for the Central Intelligence Agency, CIA, at seventeen years old. Some neighbors questioned my mother about letting me leave home at such a young age. My mother let them know that I had a job waiting for me and that God would take care of me. She has always been an inspiration to me. Also, the teaching and good deeds of my grandmother helped me. I know God shaped and molded me into the person I am today. I enjoyed traveling and beginning my new life. My desire was to work in an office in the Washington D.C. area. However, I was not eighteen years old and could not take the required polygraph test. I learned to taste foods that I was not familiar with and go to different places. I have had two biopsies for cancer, at age eighteen, but was declared to be cancer free. I am extremely thankful for God's grace and mercy that had been bestowed on me.

The Supervisors tried to make a career for me as a secretary, but I found that work was not for me. I needed more freedom to move around. I did not want to type for eight hours. Soon, I was able to accept the position of Information Control Clerk. The position required filing, which meant I could read information about people, places and events. This was the closest position I could obtain to being a spy for the CIA. Almost every student that accepted a position wanted to be a spy. However, the CIA told them to put their trench coats away. Through my position as Information Control Clerk, I learned so much. We were taught not reveal information to a person if they did not have the need to know.

The CIA had its positive effects on my life. In fact, the CIA had moral values similar to my parents. The CIA had rules about the type of persons the employees should date. Employees had to fill out a form to let them know if they had marriage plans. The CIA did not approve of drug use by the employees. However, employees were allowed a limited amount of alcohol. These rules and regulations were accepted by me, because as a child, I had acquired moral values from my parents and church leaders. Also, I wanted to please God.

This new life in the government gave me some challenges I had to overcome. My first assignment in Virginia was not the location that I wanted. However, I did well in the position and a few months later my immediate supervisor left for another position. I was qualified for the position, but was not chosen, because I was too young. I was not eighteen years old and had not taken the required polygraph test. I was not too disappointed, because I longed to be in Washington, D. C.

When I arrived in Washington, D.C., I learned and worked my way up to higher positions. I was once told by a supervisor, "you are female, black and uneducated." Further, he pointed out to me that the only thing I could change was the education. I thanked him and continued my education. I already knew that I was female and black. My father had taught me to be black and proud. I could have gone to college when I finished high school, but chose to take the Federal government job. This same supervisor gave me a gold necklace when I completed my Bachelor of Science in Cartography degree.

I remember an unkind deputy chief that knew my background training. She watched me very close and wanted to change me to a more secure area without as much freedom to move around. This was an area where security was high and persons had to go outside of this area to make or receive phone calls. In the meantime, I found favor with her immediate division chief who appreciated my work. He advised me and helped me stay in the professional area that I enjoyed. I met persons all the way to the top of the organization. This position gave me more awareness of higher opportunities. Soon, I was chosen as a CIA mentor. Through this assignment, one of my closest friends encouraged me to continue to help others.

During my first years in Washington, D.C., I searched the area with a female friend, for a church to join. After visiting many, large and small, I joined Greater People's Union Baptist Church in Southeast D.C. This church was about four miles from my job and less than a block from where I lived. In this location, I had some good times and bad times. By knowing God, I was able to get myself out of some incidents that could have alternately affected me for life. I met some young men that were kind. However, there were others that had bad intentions for my life. The unkind ones wanted to take away my possessions.

As I worked, I had acquired a savings account and brought nice items for my future apartment. Some of my female friends experienced similar situations. She gave me valuable information about men. She was married, later separated and helped me try to understand some of the situations of married life. Her daughter is my first God child. This was a nice child. I would take them out to eat and to the amusement parks in the area. My friend died from terminal cancer.

On December 23, 1988, I married my first husband. He fathered a daughter and acquired a step daughter from his previous marriage. I wanted to have a child with my husband, but he decided that he did not want any more children. This disappointed me, but I covered my feelings by showering other children with gifts and love. My step daughter caused a wedge in the marriage. I could not approve of having her move into our home on a full time basis. I did not believe in divorce, but it was the best thing for peace. Then, I continued to fill my time with helping single, separated or divorced women with their children. I enjoyed helping to make children feel happy and content.

Another friend relocated to New York and suffers from a mental condition. She had a baby during her senior year in high school and I was kind to her when she arrived in Washington, D.C. She was involved in a terrible situation at a party that caused her boyfriend to beat her in the face. She was never quite the same after this incident. She called her condition multiple sclerosis. However, I believe it was a result from the beating by her boyfriend

At the age of nineteen, I did obtain a position in the Washington, D.C. area. Finally, I was able to take the required polygraph test. While working, I began to hear of more opportunities to apply for in Washington, D.C. Soon, I began to attend College to quality for better positions. My first college was, Federal City College, which later became the University of D.C. Due to my initiative, I was chosen for a professional position as a Photogrammetrist, which involves determining measurements from photos to create maps and drawings. This position involved supporting the Photo Interpreter who was responsible for what he or she saw. The Photogrammetrist would support their work by making measurements of what was seen. The two would work together and the Photo Interpreter would reach a final conclusion. During this position, I was told that I had excellent interpersonal skills. I would find myself interacting with all types of persons. Even during flights for our work, I would talk with strangers. My co-workers would make negative comments about me talking with strangers. I let them know that through engaging strangers in conversation, I have learned that people have similar needs and thoughts. During my travels, I have seen and met many persons that look like me, with similar skin color and physical features. However, I have learned that they all are not African American, but also Mexican, Indian, Haitian, Ethiopian, Jamaican, and others. This has brought me to accept Dr. Martin Luther King Jr.'s remarks about judging people by their character and not their skin color. Throughout life, I have tried to meet each person as an individual. By not forming a prejudged determination, I accept the person for who he or she is. This approach was in my favor. I was chosen for the Project Leader position and filled in for the Branch Chief in his absence. My naturally kind spirit has been in my favor for good results from some bad situations. For example, when wrongly accused in an incident, my reputation for kindness will help resolve the situation.

I live in the Maryland area and travel to other states, where I have observed the need for more love among people. Also, through the media and reading, I am aware there is a need for more love among people in the world. I have traveled in the states and have traveled to international areas, i.e., the Bahamas, Cancun, Jamaica, and Thailand. There are so many people that are depressed, broken, confused, and seeking the abundant life. Whenever possible, I will give money or assist someone by lending a helping hand. I am able to interact with almost anyone. I say almost, because I once met a Nun while traveling for work. However, this Nun would not communicate with me. This situation taught me to be careful with people about life. I usually, will not ask probing questions, but will engage in general conversations.

By June 1995, I decided to find a Maryland church. My pastor, Rev. JM was retiring from Greater People's Union Baptist Church, my church. At this time, I had begun to want more involvement in Bible study. The red lettering in the Bible for the Four Gospels, Matthew, Mark, Luke, and John, became more interesting for me. I wanted to know more about what Jesus had said. Going to church brings stability to my life. Perhaps, because I was in church at such a young age, it really is my way of life. After visiting a few, I joined Faith Missionary Baptist Church in Largo, Maryland, where Rev. Dr. M. C. T., Sr., is the Pastor. This church has since relocated to Capitol Heights, Maryland. This church is now called The Miracle Center of Faith Missionary Baptist Church. I have attended and completed many Bible Studies, such as Going Through the Bible in One Year, Old and New Testament, Understanding God, Discipleship, and God's Great and Precious Promises. I co-taught the Experiencing God and Evangelism classes.

Call to Ministry

I witnessed hearing the voice of God during the month of November 1995. I continued to pray and listen for God's voice. On another occasion, I witnessed about a vision or dream of Jesus stepping out of my body and speaking to me. I let Jesus know that I was not worthy and asked him to return to my body. The pastor spent time in conversation with me and soon by March 21, 2000, I did my trial sermon. During the Summer Camp Program I serve as the teacher for Chapel time and the counselor for issue resolutions. There are times when I am called the Minister of Education. The classes that are noted in this spiritual journey denote certain classes that affected my life. The choices of classes give theological meaning in my life. I continue to enhance my life with religious information, for example, attending the American Baptist Churches of the South (ABCOTS) conferences, Progressive National Baptist Conference, (PNBC), and other leadership conferences, as well as attending other church services and affairs. Furthermore, I completed Spiritual Warfare, Intro to Old and New Testament, Religious Counseling, and Spiritual Man classes at the Washington Saturday College on the Howard University campus during the fall of 2000.

In the fall of 2001, I began to study for a Master of Divinity at Samuel DeWitt Proctor School of Theology at Virginia Union University, VUU. During that time, my classes were during non-traditional hours, Friday evening and Saturday morning. I was able to cross register to the Howard University Shepherd Street campus for one year of study. I received my Master of Divinity degree on, Saturday, May 9, 2005, in Richmond, Virginia. I have been able to encourage other ministers to attend the Samuel DeWitt Proctor School of Theology, at Virginia Union. Also, I have spoken with Dean K to help them enter the Master of Divinity program. I stand ready to help someone, whenever the need is apparent.

My compassion has caused me to offer pastoral care along with my pastor. Also, I assist with counseling when called upon. Women have come to me and let her know that they admire me and need help in certain situations. Usually, it is about love, because my favorite saying is, "all about love." I let them know, as my mother said, "life is not perfect." However, with God on our side, we can make it. Single women are drawn to me through their children. I can be found play adopting a child or playing God mother. I am officially a God mother to RS, a young man, who is now twenty two years old. I can be found, talking about the children dolls, playing with their toys, helping with homework, buying candy or MacDonald's burgers, giving birthday money, babysitting, and lecturing.

Outside of church, I am a substitute teacher. I enjoy speaking with the high school children about life issues. I am capable of teaching most classes and have a way about myself for inspiring the students to do their best. I remember the reports that must be written about the employee and want the students to succeed in life. The reports would evaluate the employee's performances. Also, the oral and writing skills would be rated.

During the year of April 2010 to May 2011, I served as the Executive Minister for the Faith Missionary Baptist Church at LaPlata, Maryland where I was ordained to be a Pastor. I am currently waiting to fill a position in an established church.

At this time in 2012, I am Special Assistant to the Pastor of The Miracle Center of Faith Missionary Baptist Church (MCFMBC) in Capitol Heights, Rev. Dr. M. C. T. Also, I am the President of the Minister's Council and the Sunday School Instructor for the Middle

Class students, as well as the instructor for the Wednesday Midday Bible Study. Additionally, I fill in as one of the instructors for the Tuesday and Thursday evening Bible Studies. In the midst of writing this Spiritual Autobiography, I have been assigned as the instructor for Bible Study in a senior community. Further, I am studying for a Doctor of Ministry degree at the United Theological Seminary of Dayton, Ohio. I continue to preach at my home church when called upon and preach for other churches. I serve spiritually for the Homeless ministry, and as well as the Missionary Society, and Willing Helpers Society. I continue to serve for the activities scheduled at the Charles County Nursing Rehabilitation Center in LaPlata, Maryland. Also, I am a visiting Chaplain at Doctor's Hospital in Lanham, Maryland. I provide pastoral care as a volunteer service to the hospital.

In the community, through my Faith Church, under the Social Action Ministry, I serve as the Chairperson of the Education Task-Force for the organization PRISCM, Partnership Renewal in Southern and Central Maryland. PRISCM is in place to be a voice for persons that have experienced injustices in all walks of life. The goal of PRISCM is to bring equity to all people in and around the Maryland area. In the meantime, PRISCM is a part of the Gameliel organization, located in Chicago, Illinois. This organization has many groups and members that operate internationally and throughout the United States. Also, as a member of the Clergy Caucus, I am able to assist in bringing other churches into the organization. These churches come together to gather information about injustices that may occur in each congregation. In this process, the churches are able to obtain similar issues that affect equity throughout all locations.

All my life I have been a lover of Shakespeare and I love his saying "Be not afraid of greatness: some are born great, some achieve greatness, and some have greatness thrust upon them." Overall, my mother told me that life was not going to be perfect. I have learned how to make the best of what has been thrust upon me. Through a divorce from my first husband, W.E., who was unequally yoked with me, we have grown spiritually. We had some disagreeable experiences and divorced in June 1993. However, he has grown and is now a deacon in his church. Presently, I am married to her second husband, G. S., since May 2002. We are taking one day at a time with life. Therein, I have learned to count it all joy, because my good days outweigh my bad days.

In summary, to this day, I can be found lending a hand to a single parent, lending a hand in my church, and in the community. Whenever possible I try to encourage the children that I come in contact with. During my time as a Sunday School teacher, Youth Ministry advisor, Midday Bible Study teacher and Evening Bible Study teacher for the seniors, I have been set as an example for the associate ministers.

My Church is available through the Social Action Ministry to address issues as they arise. I am the Chairperson for Education. I am available to help with pastoral care, counseling, job placement, missionary activities, homeless issues, etc. I am available to address issues at The Miracle Center of Faith Missionary Baptist Church and in the community. Also, I am the President of the Minister's Council, which is the position, to lead the Associate Ministers in the support to the Pastor of The Miracle Center of Faith Missionary Baptist Church. This position has brought light to a situation that will be addressed through the proposed project that has been generated at the United Theological Seminary for the Doctor or Ministry program. The issue of Solidifying the Relationship between the Pastor and Associate Ministers will possibly result in motivating the Associate Ministers. As the Associate Ministers learn that service to the pastor and the congregation is as important as preaching there will be possibly more harmony in the church. I believe that through Christ, these issues can be addressed and solved with positive results. I have learned to keep believing in God and to keep inspiring other people to believe.

Context Demographics

The purpose of this writing is to describe the context of the research project. The concern is historical influences, the social dynamics and population characteristics of the Prince George's County of Maryland. Past history will show that Prince George's County was a place that was known for its agricultural products. Presently, there are still some rural areas, but it is becoming more populated. The growing presence of the federal government in Maryland areas and close in the Washington D.C. and Virginia area had changed the appearance of Prince George's County. In fact, Capitol Heights of Prince George's County is twelve miles away from the White House in Washington, D.C. Therefore, it makes a great place to live in Maryland and still have some open roads and space for the living areas. Many people choose to live close to the Washington, D.C. area.

The suburbs have become popular for the shopping centers and great parking. From the People Quick Facts for Prince George's County[7], one will find that the population estimate as of 2012 is 871,500 persons. For extra information the estimated population in Maryland is 5,828,500. The land area of Prince George's County is 482.69 square miles. The overall Maryland square miles is 9,707.24. Based on the Quick Facts for Prince George's County, consider the following data: The median age is thirty four years old. The number of persons under five years old is 6.8%. The number of persons under eighteen years is 23.5%. The numbers of person's age sixty five years and over are reported as 9.8%. The female persons are 52.0%.

The racial diversity consist of White persons, 26%, Black persons, 65%, Hispanic or Latino origin, 15.2%, Asian persons, 4.3%, American Indian and Alaska Native persons, 1.0%. Native Hawaiian and other Pacific Islander persons are reported as 0.2%. Persons reporting two or more races are reported as 2.5%. The primary

---

[7]US Census Bureau State & County Quick Facts, Capitol Heights, Prince George's County,
Maryland Last modified July 1, 2015 accessed March 17, 2013 www.census.gov/quick facts.

language used in Prince George's County is English. However, Spanish is spoken by 19.8% of the population. There are 85.8% high school graduates at 25+ years of age. Those who have Bachelor degrees or higher, 25+ years of age are 29.7%.

These statistics are constantly changing, because high-tech jobs in the Prince George's County are increasing, new housing is being built, and more diverse groups of people are moving into the county. In the past 10 years property tax has increase and the cost of housing has increased. It is no longer the well-kept secret place to live at a lower price. Perhaps, the U.S. Bureau of Census has published so much in depth information that it has sparked the interest of persons living in the city and the rural areas.

Context

The research is to be conducted at The Miracle Center of Faith Missionary Baptist Church, in Capitol Heights, Maryland. In 1991, twelve founders stepped out on faith to establish the Faith Missionary Baptist Church, currently known as The Miracle Center of the Faith Missionary Baptist Church. At that time it was called the Faith Missionary Baptist Church. Only two founders remain, because God has called the others to rest or no longer in this area or the Church. Three of the original founders who are still present today are Deacon, Deaconess and the Holy Ghost.

The pastor was called to the Faith Church in February 1991. He faithfully accepted the call and God continues to do great things in his life and in the Faith Church family. Thanks can be given to God for the vision, leadership and obedience of the pastor. He continues to trust God and lead by example. He has maintained his belief in the Scriptures and God's Holy Word. It is the foundation of all his preaching and teaching. For example, an excerpt from the Affirmation of Faith, "We affirm the supremacy of the scriptures. The Bible is the guide. The Miracle Center of Faith Missionary Baptist Church is committed to the empowerment of the people through the study of

God's word."[8] The Miracle Center Church believes in "the great doctrines of the church and the Bible as God's Holy word; belief in the Triune God, The Father, The Son, and the Holy Spirit; the redemptive ministry of Jesus Christ, and the believer's resurrection made possible by the head of the Church."[9]

In December of 1999, the Faith Church moved from 122 Old Largo Road, Largo, Maryland, to the current site at 9161 Hampton Overlook, Capitol Heights, Maryland. God blessed the people to relocate and purchase the Faith Church in May, 2000. They held the Building Dedication and Cornerstone Laying Service on November 11, 2000.

The mission of the Miracle Center of Faith Missionary Baptist Church is to "exalt the Lord Jesus Christ and to spread the gospel at home and abroad. It is through the empowerment of believers through prayer, worship, education and the proclamation of the Gospel that the believers become transforming agents in a fragmented and dislocated world." [10] The Services are held every Sunday mornings, 7:30 a.m. and 10:00 a.m. and well attended by Members and Friends. Through the approximately, eighty ministries, the Miracle Center of Faith Missionary Baptist Church has found placement for approximately growing from twelve to 300 members to serve the community in the areas of Economic, Education, Empowerment, Evangelism, and Expansion, just to name a few. Over the past twenty one years, the Miracle Center Church has baptized hundreds of new converts and added new persons to a total of eight hundreds accounted for members. The church has provided structured Bible Classes, established a strong and viable Youth Ministry and licensed more than thirty five ministers to the Gospel Ministry.

---

[8]The Miracle Center of Faith Missionary Baptist Church Capitol Heights, Maryland last modified July1,2015 accessed March17,2013 www.themiraclecenterfmbc.com

[9]The Miracle Center of Faith Missionary Baptist Church Capitol Heights, Maryland.

[10]The Miracle Center of Faith Missionary Baptist Church Capitol Heights, Maryland.

The popular ministries are, Homeless Ministry, Nursing Home Ministry, Prison Ministry, Job Placement Ministry, Evangelism Ministry, Outreach Ministry, Sick Visitation Ministry, Audio and Video Ministry, Youth Ministry, Senior Ministry, Social Action Ministry, etc. The Miracle Center of Faith Missionary Baptist Church initiated a Building Fund Program that evolved into the Capital Stewardship Campaign and the Faith Fund Campaign. Presently, the church is completing a Debt Reduction Program. The celebration is planned for Sunday, January 27, 2013.

The Miracle Center of Faith Missionary Baptist Church established a ten-week Summer Youth Enrichment Program. Also, they established a weekly radio broadcast ministry. "Moments with Faith" was used to further spread the Gospel on WYCB, 1340 AM. Pastor T ordained ten ministers to the Gospel Ministry. The pastor established the Faith Missionary Baptist Church of Beltsville, Maryland as a branch for services in April 2000. Years later, he established the Waldorf, Maryland and LaPlata, Maryland branches in March 2010.

Many members secured "Faith In Action" loans to enhance the financial stability of the Faith Church; Pastor & First Lady E T, Ministers, Deacons and Deaconess' of the Faith Missionary Baptist Church. On December 31, 2001, the Faith Church refinanced the current church home for the amount of $1.9 million. The church was further blessed by members who relieved the Faith Church of financial indebtedness by assuming "Faith In Action" loans: Pastor and First Lady E T, Ministers, i.e., Rev. RS, Deacons, and Deaconess'. Records are available in the History of the Church, fmbc111.com. These have been historic moments in the life of the church, and for that, The Miracle Center of the Faith Missionary Baptist Church, say, "To God be the Glory". God ordained that the church should become "The Miracle Center" of Faith Missionary Baptist Church on November 15, 2009. The theme for 2010 was "Believe". Theme for 2012 was "Walking by Faith". The new theme for 2013 will be given during the State of the Church Address on Sunday, January 20, 2013.

In dealing with the social dynamics of this contextual analysis it is necessary to evaluate the social science research analysis to include individuals, groups, organizations of the church, the many ministries to obtain their opinions and feelings. The chosen subject is sensitive dealing with the associate ministers. It focuses mainly on the fact the preachers only want to preach. There are conclusions that are anticipated regarding the relationship between the pastor and associate ministers. In support of this project there is an attempt to find information through surveys at the Miracle Center of Faith Missionary Baptist Church of Capitol Heights, Maryland.

The Miracle Center of Faith Missionary Baptist Church are open minded individuals who can and will handle most situations that are presented before them. There are other churches that fellowship from time to time with the Miracle Center church and have been open to discussions, retreats, workshops, and other activities. These churches were available to express opinions. Further, there are those persons in and around the community that are open to surveys as they are presented. Having mixed social interactions give a mixed and varied view of subjects, which let one know that each individual has a right to his or her own opinion. Therefore, the survey has been presented, but opinions are still ongoing.

The male associate ministers serve as stand in father images. The female associate ministers are the stand in mothers. Also, the special assistant to the pastor serves as a stand in mother. The deacons, deaconess and trustees serve as fill in uncles and aunts to the children. Overall, the entire church, including lay persons serves as nurturers to the children. At this level the associate ministers are involved. However, training is on-going to keep service as a priority. Pastor will let all persons know that if they see a need, just do it. The Miracle Center of Faith Missionary Baptist Church believes in the scriptures. The suggestions or commands let the associate ministers know that service is required.

The Miracle Center of Faith Missionary Baptist Church constantly stands ready as a society to help the congregation learn and grow from their experiences. Also, children learn by example, so if the parent can be a good role model for them. In the church atmosphere, women had repairs made for no charge. For example, earlier this year, during Hurricane Sandy, repairs were made in basement walls that leaked every time it rained. Imagine helping female or possibly males in need, according to information from the U. S. census website, households, and 4,028,000 male single households (or over 16,715,000 single parent families in the U.S.) which could be male or female. For further information, check the US census website at www.census.gov. This information is used by the church to determine which ministries are required. For example, the youth ministry, missionary, women or men's ministry can address situations that occur. Not much is detailed about the single male, unless he becomes homeless. The focus is primarily on the female, because she is considered weaker. These are situations when associate ministers can become involved. The Miracle Center of Faith Missionary Baptist Church does a fine job of looking out for the male along with the female persons.

In summary, one of the disadvantages of The Miracle Center is to offer the local social service as a good source of support. However, the church should be a primary source. This context analysis has examined the issue of concern in the Capitol Heights, Maryland area.

For reference, Appendix E will provide a sample of statistics. One of the most significant challenges is choosing the ministry to best fit the needed service. These issues present challenges, opportunities for learning and growing. There are persons that are willing to assist senior citizens. The Miracle Center of Faith Missionary Baptist Church recommends exercise to deal with stress. They use relaxation techniques, watching movies, going for walks and light exercise. The congregation is known for fellowship events that include singing and dancing. They try to mix with other adults who can help with childcare. In the Prince George's County there are Army Divisions of Bolling Air Force Base and Andrews AFB. There are Supermarkets, such as, Giant Food, Safeway, Aldi, Save-a-lot, Shoppers and Food Lion. Also, I am usually the hospitality chairperson for most events.

In reading *Studying Congregations: A New Handbook,* by Nancy Ammerman, it was useful as a reference for pastors, leaders, planning groups. It provided a way to analyze the congregation. Being able to look around the congregation and some issues that needed to be addressed became apparent. For example, the thought about doing research on simply, it's good to know Jesus. The book *Studying Congregations* can be helpful to continue to preach at every given opportunity. I enjoy doing research about whatever subject the Lord places in my spirit. The congregation appears to look forward to hearing the preached word. Preaching will encourage and inspire the listeners and leave them feeling blessed. However, it is apparent that service at church is needed.

CHAPTER TWO

BIBLICAL FOUNDATIONS

The aim of the biblical foundations is to set forth a model of ministry entitled, Solidifying the Relationship between the Pastor and Associate Ministers. The model addresses the ingredients necessary to deal with incongruences between the pastor and associate ministers as it relates to their roles and responsibilities. The population includes eighteen associate ministers within the age range eighteen to seventy two years old. Both texts show forth the presence of a structure for solidifying the relationship of subordinates to leadership. The context lacks such a structure for the targeted demographic. In essence, the ministry focuses on promoting harmony between pastor and associate ministers.

Old Testament Foundation

The Old Testament scripture is Numbers 12:1-11, NIV and it states, Miriam and Aaron began to talk against Moses because of his Cushite wife, for he had married a Cushite.²"Has the LORD spoken only through Moses?" they asked. "Hasn't he also spoken through us?" And the LORD heard this. ³(Now Moses was a very humble man, more humble than anyone else on the face of the earth.)⁴At once the LORD said to Moses, Aaron and Miriam, "Come out to the tent of meeting, all three of you." So the three of them went out.⁵Then the LORD came down in a pillar of cloud; he stood at the entrance to the tent and summoned Aaron and Miriam. When the two of them stepped forward, ⁶ he said, "Listen to my words: "When there is a prophet among you, I, the LORD, reveal myself to them in visions, I speak to them in dreams.⁷ But this is not true of my servant Moses; he is faithful in all my house.⁸ With him I speak face to face, clearly and not in riddles; he sees the form of the LORD. Why then were you not afraid to speak against my servant Moses?"⁹ The anger of the LORD burned against them, and he left them.¹⁰ When the cloud lifted from above the tent, Miriam's skin was leprous[a]—it became as white as snow. Aaron turned toward her and saw that she had a defiling skin disease,¹¹and he said to Moses, "Please, my lord, I ask you not to hold against us the sin we have so foolishly committed. ¹

Introduction

The Holy Scriptures are the basis for showing how a leader must realize that followers are not always pleased. Numbers 12: 1-10 will become the primary source that lead the thoughts presented. Dr. Thomas L. Constable presents, "The title the Jews used in their Hebrew Old Testament for this book comes from the fifth word in the book in the Hebrew text, 'bemidbar: ' in the wilderness."[2] "This is, of course, appropriate since the Israelites spent most of the time covered in the narrative of Numbers in the wilderness."[3]

Contextual Analysis

In view of Scriptural support for Mosaic authorship for whole of the Pentateuch in view of the intimately close association of Leviticus with the Book of Exodus where it explicitly states that Moses wrote down all that Yahweh said), (Exodus 24:4 it is reasonable to assume Mosaic authorship of the book of Numbers and Leviticus."[4] "Nevertheless, Mosaic authorship is assumed. Support for this assumption is presented in the Introduction to the Pentateuch."[5] De Canio reports,

Some biblical scholars contend that the Book of Numbers is not easy to analyze, or to outline because the contents of the material appear varied and the arrangement of the material seems to lack a literary sense of unity and coherence that is characteristic of a "book" (Allen 1990:670). However, when the Book of Numbers is viewed from the broad sense of Israel's rebellions and God's assurances that the covenant, though interrupted, has not failed, a pattern of material organization emerges that displays coherence.[6]

---

[1] Numbers 12:1-11. NIV
[2] Thomas L. Constable, *Notes on Numbers* 2016 Edition Introduction accessed October 2014 www.soniclight.com/constable/notes/htm/OT/Numbers/Numbers.htm
[3] Thomas L. Constable, *Notes on Numbers* 2016 Edition Introduction.
[4] Frank DeCanio, *From the series:* Pentateuch, an Analysis and Synthesis Bible.org.
[5] Frank DeCanio, *From the series:* Pentateuch, an Analysis and Synthesis.
[6] Frank DeCanio, *From the series:* Pentateuch, an Analysis and Synthesis.

The Book of Leviticus completes the Book of Exodus and forms a historical and theological bridge to the Book of Numbers and beyond that to the Book of Deuteronomy, for the historical and theological presuppositions found in the last two books of the Pentateuch are rooted in the Books of Exodus and Leviticus.[7] DeCanio continues, "The historical context of the Book of Numbers is a part of the larger historical context for the Pentateuch. Although it follows Leviticus both chronologically and canonically its historical context is more immediate with the end of Exodus and the beginning of Deuteronomy."[8] Finally, DeCanio discusses,

The socio-cultural context of Numbers begins where Exodus and Leviticus end—Israel is encamped at Sinai. However, by the start of chapter 20, Israel has moved on to the region of Kadesh. From that point on the nation wanders in the wilderness for the next thirty-eight plus years, eventually ending up on the Plains of Moab across the Jordan opposite Jericho. Throughout these thirty-eight years, the people live a nomadic lifestyle as they move from place to place. Although their covenant-relationship with Yahweh has been disturbed, it has not been terminated. As a result, Israelite society is yet bound by the stipulations of the Mosaic Covenant. As significant and complex is this socio-cultural context, it has little effect on understanding the theological message of Numbers, other than that it is part of the contextual framework within which that message is developed.[9]

The literary genre and structure of the book of Numbers, discussed by Nubian mercenaries, during 1470 BC, record, "The book of Numbers is made up of several different types of literatures. There are laws, history accounts, prayers, prophecy, wilderness sceneries, and more. In large measure, however, the book may be described, similarly to Exodus and Leviticus, as law embedded in a narrative of theological history.

---

[7] Frank DeCanio, *From the series:* <u>Pentateuch, an Analysis and Synthesis</u>.
[8] Frank DeCanio, *From the series:* <u>Pentateuch, an Analysis and Synthesis</u>.
[9] Frank DeCanio, *From the series:* <u>Pentateuch, an Analysis and Synthesis.</u>

J. D. Douglas and Merrill C. Tenney does an overview of Numbers, stating, "The author is anonymous, but comments else in the Bible seem to support the traditional view that Moses is responsible for the Pentateuch as a whole."[10] Secondly, "The initial composition of the book must have taken place at the end of the wilderness wanderings (either late in the fifteenth or early in the thirteenth cent. B.C.; those who reject Mosaic authorship usually date the book after the Exile, while acknowledging that much of the material is several centuries earlier)."[11]

Third, Douglas and Tenney, state, "The purpose of Numbers is to provide a historical-theological account of the Israelite wanderings, beginning with their departure from SINAI, stressing their unfaithfulness in the wilderness, and ending with their arrival in the plains of MOAB; to encourage the new generation to remain faithful to God and thus to prepare themselves to conquer the Promised Land."[12] Finally, the contents addressed as,

Organization of the people for their march into the wilderness (Num. 1-4); sanctification of the people and beginning of their march (chs. 5-10); complaints and rebellion of the people (chs. 11-19); events during the last stage of the wanderings (chs. 20-25); preparation of the new generation to possess the Promised Land (chs. 26-36).[13]

Cited in the book of Numbers there is an issue of insubordination as displayed in their wilderness experience between Miriam and Aaron against Moses. Miriam and Aaron are subordinates to Moses, the leader. In an effort to support our presupposition, we will do an analysis of the book of Numbers. The Scriptures, Numbers 12:1, informs that God was not pleased with Aaron and Miriam. Further, in verse 3, it is written that Moses was a humble man, (Now the man Moses was very humble, more than all men who were on the face of the earth.) God let Aaron and Miriam know that the vision was given to Moses as the leader.

---

[10] J. D. Douglas and Merrill C. Tenney, *Zondervan Illustrated Bible Dictionary* (Grand Rapids, MI: Zondervan, 1987), 1029-1031.

[11] J. D. Douglas and Merrill C. Tenney, *Zondervan Illustrated Bible Dictionary*.

[12] J. D. Douglas and Merrill C. Tenney, *Zondervan Illustrated Bible Dictionary*.

[13] J. D. Douglas and Merrill C. Tenney, *Zondervan Illustrated Bible Dictionary*.

Don Fleming discusses Miriam and Aaron's jealousy. He states,

> Apparently Moses' first wife had died and he had remarried. His new wife was not an Israelite, and Miriam and Aaron used this as an excuse to criticize him. The real reason for their attack, however, was their jealousy of Moses' status as supreme leader of Israel. Moses, being a humble man, did not defend himself, because he knew that God was the only true judge; and God's judgment was although Aaron, Miriam and the seventy had a part in the leadership of Israel, Moses' position was unique. God spoke with him directly and entrusted him with supreme authority over his people (12:1-8).[14]

Miriam possibly was punished, because God knew that Moses was a humble man. "God did, but just as a daughter who had been publicly rebuked by her father had to spend seven days in shame, so did Miriam."[15] According to Leviticus 14:8, "the person to be cleansed must wash their clothes, shave off all their hair and bathe with water; then they will be ceremonially clean. After this they may come into the camp, but they must stay outside their tent for seven days."[16]

It appears that Miriam was indeed a leader, but not on a level as Moses with God. However, Miriam must have had enough spiritual connection to God, perhaps, through vision or dreams to become jealous of Moses. Also, by overseeing for Moses while he was in the Nile and rescued by Pharaoh's daughter, Miriam must have believed she should be in line to God before Moses. Being in a leadership position can cause followers to believe they should be higher than the leader.

The guidelines will focus on biblical interpretation with focus on the spiritual aspect. Then the Scriptures will be explained in a practical

---

[14]Don Fleming, *Concise BIBLE COMMENTARY* (Chattanooga, TN: AMG Publishers, 1988), 69.

[15]Don Fleming, *Concise BIBLE COMMENTARY*, 69.

[16]Don Fleming

way to show have a leader can handle the same type of situation today. What the model represent from this text is based on how Moses dealt with the people, along with his brother, Aaron, and sister, Miriam. The objective of the Biblical Foundations is to present a model of ministry entitled Solidifying the relationship between the Pastor and Associate Ministers. From a homiletics point of view by Spence and Excell, in *The Pulpit Commentary*, view Numbers 12: 1-10 as the contradiction of sinners. It states,

We have in this chapter, spiritually, the contradiction of the Jews against their brother after the flesh; morally, the sin and punishment of jealously and envy in high places. Consider, therefore, first, That as Moses is the type of him who was the mediator of a better covenant, who was meek and lowly in heart; so Aaron and Miriam, when arrayed against Moses, represent the Levitical priesthood at the time of our Lord, and the Jewish synagogue, in their carnal pride and exclusiveness.[17] "Nor is this typical character arbitrary or unreal, for we may clearly see in them the same tendencies which afterwards ripened into utter blasphemy and Decide."[18]

Second, that Miriam and Aaron justified their opposition to Moses by dwelling upon their own spiritual authority. Even so the synagogue and priesthood of the Jews magnified themselves against the Lord's Christ and their own Messiah, on the ground that they themselves were commissioned of God.[19]

Third, Spence continued to show that God would intervene to for a faithful servant as he did for Moses. Also, God vindicated his holy servant Jesus against all the blasphemy of the Jews and give him a name above every name. Finally, Spence discussed,

God interfered to punish Miriam with leprosy for her pride and rancor. Even so the synagogue of the Jews became the synagogue of

---

[17] H. D. M. Spence and Joseph S. Exell, *The Pulpit Commentary Volume 2 Leviticus Numbers* (Grand Rapids, MI: Wm. B. Eerdmans Publishing Co.) p. 129, 130.

[18] H. D. M. Spence and Joseph S. Exell, *The Pulpit Commentary Volume 2 Leviticus Numbers*, 130.

[19] H. D. M. Spence and Joseph S. Exell, *The Pulpit Commentary Volume 2 Leviticus Numbers*, 131

Satan, and they themselves are in exile, political and religious, until they shall cry for mercy to their Brother, the one Mediator.[20]

In further research, it was revealed that Moses waited to appoint Joshua. Nevertheless, the focus is on the relationship between Moses, Aaron, and Miriam. Aaron was chosen to be the spoke person, Assistant to Moses. From research, it was shown that Miriam is Moses' older sister and was chosen as the music person. Perhaps, by being Moses older sister and the person responsible for the music, which set the atmosphere, she felt, somewhat over Moses. Also, since she was the one who sat Moses in the Nile to save his life from Pharaoh, she felt that God should speak to her. As with the pastor at the context Church, the model addresses the needs of the pastor of The Miracle Center of FMBC. The pastor is tasked with ways to motivate the associate ministers to a higher level, while letting them know their positions. The morale is low and the associate ministers are standing in line, waiting for a schedule to preach. However, this is not acceptable to the pastor and other plans are being generated to find better ways for them to serve as associate ministers. There have been times when certain associate ministers have felt that they deserve higher positions or should be favored to move outside to other churches. The pastor does have authority to meet with other pastors and discuss church openings or paid positions that can be filled by the associate ministers. These situations create competition and usually, there is a rift in the membership. For example, when Miriam became jealous of Moses, she caused Aaron to relook at the marriage of Moses and later he took authority to create the golden calf. Miriam perhaps, recognized that Moses new wife was "an Ethiopian woman—Hebrew, "a Cushite woman"—Arabia was usually called in Scripture the land of Cush, its inhabitants being descendants of that son of Ham (see on [77] Ex 2:15) and being accounted generally a vale and contemptible race (see on [78] Am 9:7)."[21] Aaron deserved as much punishment as Miriam, but

---

[20] H. D. M. Spence and Joseph S. Exell, *The Pulpit Commentary Volume 2 Leviticus Numbers*, 131.

[21] Jamieson-Fausett-Brown, *Commentary on the Whole Bible* (New York, NY:

God spared him and he asked Moses to spare Miriam. From research, it is said, "Feminine jealously and ambition were the drawbacks of her otherwise commanding character."[22] Also, Miriam was considered as the chief instigator in the jealously against Moses. In most situations, involving the pastor and associate ministers, there is a lead person who stirs the negative concern, and begins the change in morale of others.

The Old Testament scriptures relating to Moses, his brother, Aaron, and his sister, Miriam, can be used as a model to show that the Pastor and followers do not have a perfect relationship. By taking the study of Moses as the leader and Aaron, along with Miriam as followers, one will find that followers will react to the leader. The choice of Moses, along with his older brother, Aaron and his sister Miriam, one may say, why not Joshua? Most persons would use Joshua, because he became the second leader after Moses. However, followers should be considered, because they affect the leader. Moses let Joshua be in the "tent of the meeting,"[23] where the presence of God was powerful. Moses knew he would die and therefore, he tried to prepare Joshua for the future.

In further research, it was revealed that Moses waited until the last day of his life to appoint Joshua. This remark is up for farther discussion as the pending project progress.

In support of the project www.aish.com was used with information based on Numbers 27:12, "And the Lord said unto Moses, Get thee up into this mount Abarim, and see the land which I have given unto the children of Israel." Then in verse 18, "And the Lord said unto Moses, Take thee Joshua the son of Nun, a man in whom is the spirit, and lay thine hand upon him; 19 "And set him before Eleazar the priest, and before all the congregation; and give him a charge in their sight. Then verse 20, "And thou shalt put some of thine honour upon him, that all the congregation of the children of Israel may be obedient." For further

---

Zondervan Publishers), 1999, 118-150.

[22] Andrew Robert Fausett M.A., D.D., *"Definition for "Miriam" Fausett's Bible Dictionary"*. (Fausett's), 1878, 91.

[23] Exodus 33:11, King James Version. Unless otherwise noted, all scripture references in this document are from the NIV.

information, Deuteronomy 31: 1-2, "And Moses went and spake these words unto all Israel. 2 And he said unto them, I am an hundred and twenty years old this day; I can no more go out and come in: also the Lord hath said unto me, Thou shalt not go over this Jordan." For further detail on Joshua, verse 7 can be used, "And Moses called unto Joshua, and said unto him in the sight of all Israel, Be strong and of a good courage: for thou must go with this people unto the land which the Lord hath sworn unto their fathers to give them; and thou shalt cause them to inherit it." In support of the research, the Torah ideas dealt with 40 years in the desert, maintaining that "Joshua subordinated himself to Moses." Joshua was known as the only one waiting patiently at the foot of Mount Sinai. Joshua and Caleb are the only spies who did not rebel against Moses. They urged to enter the land of Israel. When others appeared to challenge Moses by saying they looked like "grasshoppers" Joshua rushed to Moses defense. Joshua appeared to appreciate the greatness of Moses. Therefore, before Moses died, he chose Joshua and God approved the choice. God's trust in Joshua to make choices is said to be "the first use of man's free will." "This is considered as God's greatest gift to man, the ultimate expression of his trust."[24] In the book, *A Historical Journey into Biblical times, 12 Tribes, 10 Plagues, the 2 Men Who were Moses*, it becomes apparent that history and biblical can relate. For example, Phillips, Graham's book, *A Historical Journey into Biblical times. 12 Tribes 10 Plagues the 2 Men who were Moses.* Let's one know,

This book is an historical investigation into the birth of the ancient Israelite religion upon which today monotheistic faiths are based." "Monotheism is arguably the single most influential concept in the history of humanity, but from the historian's perspective its origins in ancient Canaan around 3,500 years ago are still shrouded in mystery.[25]

---

[24]Graham Phillips, *A Historical Journey into Biblical Times, 12 Tribes, 10 Plagues, the 2 Men Who were Moses:* (Berkeley, CA: Seastone Press, 2003), 92.
[25]Graham Phillips, *A Historical Journey into Biblical Times.*

Through Graham Phillips research, he began to believe that Old Testament was "closer to the truth than many historians have previously believed, and biblical episodes which skeptics consider to be little more than myths were in fact a series of remarkable historical events."[26] The monotheism confesses one God. Phillips research, that even the Judaism, Christianity, and the Islam religions confirm certain Scriptures and acknowledgement of the one God. The Jewish use the "Shema" which contains, Chapter 6, verses 4 to 7 in the biblical Book of Deuteronomy as the most important commandment. Second, likewise the Christians use Chapter 12, verses 28 to 30 of the New Testament of Mark, to note that Jesus said the most important commandment was... "Hear O Israel: The Lord our God is one Lord: And thou shalt love the Lord thy God with all thy heart, and with all thy soul, and with all thy mind, and with all thy strength:" this is the first commandment. Further, the Islamic call to prayer in the "Adhan" is the same words for one God.

While speaking with God, Moses let God know that he did not speak well. God let Moses know that Aaron could speak for him. Miriam was not placed in a position, but she was Moses' sister. From research, Miriam is credited with placing Moses in the river (Nile) to avoid death as a young new born child. Imagine, she and Moses' mother having to live and watch Moses grow under the Egyptian household principles. This must have been difficult, because they knew that Moses was a Hebrew, just like she and his brother and her mother. One wonders, what made Moses know that the Egyptian rule and power over the Hebrew/Israelite people was wrong? After Moses killed the Egyptian, he fled the land, to escape his Egyptian, so called, father and brother, his journey changed his life and he became a follower of God. His journey to Mt. Sinai would change his life forever and changed the lives of all people, who would believe in honoring the Ten Commandments. Who would know that his life would to this day affect all moral values?

---

[26]Graham Phillips, *A Historical Journey into Biblical Times*.

When Moses married Jethro's daughter, of a different culture, Miriam, his sister, became troubled. Aaron and Miriam are examples of followers not agreeing with the leader. The vision from God that the leader receives is not always clear, even to the leader. Leaders have been known to question God and sometimes do not let the followers know that God has spoken to him or her. In many cases, the leader has issues in relating what God has spoken to the followers. Aaron and Miriam did not understand Moses' communication with God. While Moses was on Mt. Sinai receiving the Ten Commandments, Aaron and Miriam were speaking against him. Imagine, Aaron creating the golden image, the calf, opposing the Godly image. The scriptures, Exodus 20:5,"Thou shall have no other gods before me," can be used to show God's displeasure with Aaron and Miriam as followers. Clearly, for confirmation God does give the vision to the leader and others must follow. Based on Proverbs 29:18, "Where there is no vision, the people perish:" Also, it is clear that God will punish a follower that does not accept the vision from the leader. Consider Miriam turned snow-white with leprosy as a punishment from God. However, Moses love for his sister, caused him to ask God to forgive her and restore wholeness to her.

As Jethro and Moses communicated together, Jethro suggested to Moses to choose a number of priests and elders to assist him and follow after Aaron. The scriptures, Exodus 24:13, verify that Moses referred to Joshua as his minister. For example, "And Moses rose up, and his minister Joshua: and Moses went up into the mount of God." "Moses gave the Torah to Joshua as a final gesture. Phillips states, "The Torah in the hands of the Sages to interpret and clarify according to the rules of derivation that God commanded to Moses. Prophets then can admonish and warn the people, but they cannot introduce new laws. Torah is not in Heaven."[27]

Imagine, as the Biblical Foundation is shaped, one tend to look back for over 2,000 years based on the birth of Christ. However, as the

---

[27]Graham Phillips, *A Historical Journey into Biblical Times: 12 Tribes 10 plagues the 2 Men who were Moses* (Berkeley, CA: Ulysses Press), 2003, 118-150.

influences of time come toward the present time, there are names that become influences. For example, Dr. Martin Luther King, Jr. can be mentioned for his influence on peace and love. Jesus told his Disciples of the greatest commandment to be that they "love one another" and he had loved them. Therefore, Dr. King, Jr., continues the love of one another. In support of Biblical foundation research the book, *"Spiritual Leaders Who Changed the World"* by Dr. Robert Coles, one would point a few, such as, Elijah Mohammad, Desmond Tutu, Mary Daly, and William J. Seymour, as persons, who, 'shook thing up". In fact, Mary Daly, who stirred up the feminist movement, born in 1928 is still alive. She identified certain ways that the Catholic Church showed oppression of women. Daly challenged the name or noun of the term "God". She believed that "God is a Be-ing". Further, there are some, especially women, who are known to use her expression, 'live, move, and have our being.'"[28]

In dealing with leadership style; Why did Moses wait until the last day of his life to appoint Joshua? It was apparent that Joshua was a leader in the Amalek battle. Then to Joshua credit for leadership is the ability to humble himself to one who is greater. The priests were responsible for the sacrifices in the morning and evening. As the religion progressed, in later books of the Bible, King David wanted to build a temple for God and take care of the offerings and sacrifices. However, blood was on his hands for murder and he could not build the temple. Later, Solomon built the temple for the sacrifice purposes and God was pleased with him. Throughout Old Testament, the sacrifice of animal blood was the form of religion and persons believed they were forgiven for sins.

Some followers do not believe that the pastor receives visions from God. When the pastor uses the term, divine revelation, some believers are in doubt. Many have expressed the fact that God has not spoken to them, so they do not believe. There are courses that are taught to teach persons to acknowledge and recognize that God does speak to them.

---

[28]Ira Rifkin and Robert Coles, *Spiritual Leaders Who Changed the World: The Essential Handbook to the Past Century of Religion* (Woodstock, VT: Skylight Paths Publishing), 2008, 102-125.

48

"There is a Christian Leadership University that offers a course, REN 103 Communion with God that can guide one through the process of hearing from God and communicating with him."[29] Also, one can learn from Ecclesiastes 5:2, that prayer is a way that God can do most of the talking for us. God's word is a base for prayer when used to remind God of what is expected and things that have been promised to the believer.

In support of the project research of the book, *Biblical Foundation for Baptist Churches: A Contemporary Ecclesiology* by John S. Hammett, the Church should be shaped "by the biblical mandate of God."[30] However, Hammett does the Scriptures to deal with theology and Baptist history. Further, it is written that sociologist use the term, literalism" to deal with biblical interpretation. The Gallup survey reports, "There is three in 10 Americans that interpret ate the Bible literally, as the actual word of God." Research shows that 49% of Americans say the Bible is the inspired word of God. This percent believe that the Bible should not be taken literally. Then there are 17% that believe the Bible is just ancient stories written by men. The other 34 % were not defined for their beliefs and farther research will come forth at a later date.

Detailed Analysis

The Holy Bible Scriptures are used as the primary source for references and research. Originally, King James Version, KJV, is chosen first. However, for this project New International Version, NIV, is documented for clearer understanding. Also, New Revised Standard Version, NRSV, is used for clarification. Further, various Commentaries are used to verify Scriptures. From a homiletics view,

---

[29]Christian Leadership University, Access date March 2014 www.CLUonline.com Hear God's voice-2.htm. John S. Hammett,

[30]*Biblical Foundations for Baptist Churches: A Contemporary Ecclesiology* (Goshen, IN: Kregel Publication), 2005, 67-108.

Biblical Foundations for Baptist Churches: A Contemporary Ecclesiology (Goshen, IN: Kregel Publication), 2005, 67-108.

H. D. M. Spence and Joseph S. Exell bring clarity to the fact that God does forgive in Numbers1: 3. Note this quote, titled wrath awaked and wrath appeased. "In this short passage we have, in a microcosm, the whole sad history of the Church. For the history of the Church, as it is glorious on the side of God and his faithfulness, so it is sad indeed on the side of man and his unfaithfulness. Here we may see trial followed at once by failure, temptation by sin; failure and sin followed by fiery wrath. Yet wrath is never without mercy, for the fire is quenched by the voice of the mediator."[31] According to Bible Chronology, "The dates given in the bible concerning the events surrounding the exodus period reveal that Moses was using a *lunar calendar*. This lunar calendar was basically the same as that used today in modern Israel.[1] Nevertheless, working in harmony with the lunar calendar, it is equally evident that the *360 calendar* was *also* being used, at least *ideally*. (This is demonstrably true whether or not Moses was personally aware of it. Indeed, likely Moses was aware of it; the Israelites had just left the land of Egypt where a variation of the 360 calendar was already in use.)"[32]

David Noel Freedman states, " Miriam, a woman in Israel's wilderness community who exercised religious leadership alongside Moses and Aaron (Mic 6:4). Introduced as prophetess and Aaron's sister, Miriam led the women in the celebration at the Sea (Exod 15:20-21) and joined Aaron in a rebellion against Moses, for which she was punished with leprosy (Num 12:1-15; cf. Deut 24:9). ... listed as the sister of Aaron and Moses. According to Num 20:1, she died and was buried at Kadesh. In Num 12: 1-15 different layers of tradition present Miriam and Aaron raising controversies with Moses regarding his Cushite wife and his authority in rendering God's word. The latter controversy clearly reflects a crisis of religious leadership. The account seeks to establish the primacy of Moses as God's spokesperson, but in doing so it does not negate the authenticity of

---

[31]H. D. M. Spence and Joseph S. Exell, *The Pulpit Commentary: volume 2 Leviticus Numbers* (Grands Rapids, MI: Wm. B. Eerdmans Publishing Co., 1980), 103.

[32] Bible-prophecy.org, Access dated March 2014 Bible Chronology and numeric patterns from Creation to the Flood--- to the Exodus.

Miriam and Aaron as meditators of God's word."[33] H. D. M. Spence and Joseph S. Exell, states,

The Sedition and Punishment of Miriam. Verse 1.—And Miriam and Aaron spake against Moses. While the people were encamped at Hazeroth, and therefore probably very soon after the events of the last chapter. That Miriam's was the moving spirit in the matter is sufficiently evident, (1) because her name stands first; (2) because the verb "spake" is in the feminine, "and she said"); (3) because the ground of annoyance was a peculiarly feminine one, a mésalliance; (4) because Miriam alone was punished; (5) because Aaron never seems to have taken the lead in anything. He appears uniformly as a man of weak and pliable character, who was singularly open to influence from others for good or for evil.[34]

Like Aaron, there are persons who may be "superior"[35] to the leading person in certain gifts. Spence, states, that Aaron, seemed to have "a general discontent at the manifest inferiority of his position inclined him to take up her quarrel (Miriam's) and to echo her complaints."[36] However, both Miriam and Aaron should have considered that when Jethro, the priest of Midian, Moses' father-in-law, heard of all that God had done for Moses, they would respect Moses. Further, Jethro had counsel with Moses and gave him advice on how to change his "current approach"[37] with the children of Israel. Jethro realized, "The problem was simply that the job was too big for Moses to do. His energies were spent unwisely, and justice was delayed for many in Israel."[38] First, Jethro told Moses to listen to him and that God would be with him. He stated, "Stand before God for the

---

[33] David Noel Freedman, *The Anchor Bible Dictionary Volume 4 K-N* (New York, NY: Doubleday), 1922, 869-870.

[34] H. D. M. Spence and Joseph S. Exell, *The Pulpit Commentary Volume 2 Leviticus Numbers* (Grand Rapids, MI: Wm. B. Eerdmans Publishing Co.), 129-130.

[35] H. D. M. Spence and Joseph S. Exell, *The Pulpit Commentary Volume 2 Leviticus Numbers*, 129.

[36] H. D. M. Spence and Joseph S. Exell, *The Pulpit Commentary Volume 2 Leviticus Numbers*, 129.

[37] Ask.com Exodus 18:17-18.

[38] Ask.com Exodus 18:19-20.

people, so that you may bring the difficulties to God. And you shall teach them the statues and the laws, and show them the way in which they must walk and the work they must do." This was the first step for Moses with the people. It was considered as "delegation."[39] Further, Moses had to pray for the people, bring difficulties to God, teach them the statues and the laws. Then, Jethro advised Moses to "delegate the responsibility of resolving disputes."[40]

Jethro stated, "Moreover you shall select from all the people able men, such as fear God, men of truth, hating covetousness; and place such over them to be rulers of thousands, rulers of hundreds, rulers of fifties, and rulers of tens. And let them judge the people at all times. Then it will be that every great matter they shall bring to you, but every small matter they themselves shall judge. So it will be easier for you, for they will bear the burden with you.[41]

If Miriam and Aaron had followed the leadership of Moses as delegated, stayed within their roles, then the following, their situation would not exist:

Based on the writing of Spurgeon, as stated, "There is a clear analogy between the leadership of Moses for Israel and the leadership of a pastor among God's people. The analogy does not fit at every point, but in many aspects:

- God was recognized as the true leader of the people.
- The leader could not do the work of leadership alone.
- The leader had a special responsibility for prayer and teaching.
- The leader must select, train, and give authority to others to help in the work.
- The people had a definite role in all this (Deuteronomy 1:13)"[42]

---

[39]Ask.com Exodus 18:19-20.
[40]Ask.com Exodus 18:21-22.
[41]Ask.com Exodus 18:21-22.
[42]Exodus 18:19-20.

From the title Dissension of Aaron and Miriam, Ray Comfort states, "Then Miriam and Aaron spoke against Moses because of the Ethiopian woman whom he had married; for he had married an Ethiopian woman. So they said, "Has the Lord indeed spoken only through Moses? Has He not spoken through us also?"[43] And the Lord heard it. (Now the man Moses was very humble, more than all men who were on the face of the earth.) Suddenly the Lord said to Moses, Aaron, and Miriam, "Come out, you three, to the tabernacle of meeting!" [44]So the three came out. The Lord came down in the pillar of cloud and stood in the door of the tabernacle, and called Aaron and Miriam. And they both went forward. Then He said,

> Hear now My words: If there is a prophet among you, I, the Lord, make Myself known to him in a vision; I speak to him in a dream. Not so with My servant Moses; He is faithful in all My house. I speak with him face to face, Even plainly, and not in dark sayings; And he sees the form of the Lord. Why then were you not afraid? To speak against My servant Moses?[45]

So the anger of the Lord was aroused against them, and He departed. And when the cloud departed from above the tabernacle, suddenly Miriam became leprous, as white as snow."[46] In Comfort's discussion, he states, "God Himself said that Moses was His "faithful servant."[47] What an unspeakably high honor-- to be called a faithful servant. These are the words that we should all live to hear on the day we stand before the Lord, "Well done, good and faithful servant." (Matt.25:23)"[48] Also, Comfort discussed and wrote of the desire of the Israelites for meat in Chapter 11. He stated, "[49] As for the people, God

---

[43]Ray Comfort, *The Evidence Bible: New King James Version NKJV* (Alachua, FL: Bridge-Logos, 2011), 12.
[44]Ray Comfort, *The Evidence Bible: New King James Version NKJV.*
[45] Ray Comfort, *The Evidence Bible: New King James Version NKJV.*
[46]Ray Comfort, *The Evidence Bible: New King James Version NKJV.*
[47]Ray Comfort, *The Evidence Bible: New King James Version NKJV.*
[48]Ray Comfort, *The Evidence Bible: New King James Version NKJV.*
[49]Ray Comfort, *The Evidence Bible: New King James Version NKJV.*

said they would have plenty of meat to eat. He would send them enough meat to make them sick of it. They would have it for a whole month."[50] Douglas MacCallum and LindsayJudisch continue the discussion, stating, ", that all of It appears, actually the developments recorded in Numbers 11 took place in the same location, even though the name "Taberah" occurs in verse 3 and the name "Kibroth-Hattaavah" appears in verses 34-35. There is, firstly, no mention of a move to a new campsite until the end of the chapter (in verse 35). Nor, secondly, does any campsite intervene in the general itinerary of Numbers 33 between the Wilderness of Sinai and Kibroth-Hattaavah (verse 16). The name "Taberah" applied, in all likelihood, only to the one end of the campsite which was destroyed by the fire dispatched by the Lord as an initial warning of worse to come if carping continued in Israel (verse 1). It was only this one specific sector of the site which was called "Taberah" (which is to say "Burning") by virtue of the burning which consumed the tents which had been pitched within its confines (verse 3)."[51]

In support of the project, John Goldingay states, "God did put onto seventy senior Israelites some of the spirit that was on Moses (which need not imply he had less). The sign is that they "prophesy," which means something like speaking in tongues, a sign for them and the community that God's spirit has come upon them and they can share in Moses responsibly."   With this support in mind, one can understand that of the seventy someone may feel the need for more empowerment. For example, based on Numbers 12: 1-10, Goldingay, states, "Miriam and Aaron spoke against Moses in connection with the Ethiopian wife he had taken: "He has taken an Ethiopian wife!" They said, "Has Yahweh really only spoken through Moses? Has he not spoken through us?" Yahweh heard." Goldingay continues, to show that Yahweh was not pleased with Aaron and Miriam. He states, Yahweh asked them, why were you not afraid to speak against my servant Moses? So Yahweh's anger flared against them. He went away, and as

---

[50] Ray Comfort, *The Evidence Bible: New King James Version NKJV*.
[51] Douglas MacCallum and Lindsay Judisch, *The reading from the Old Testament: Nineteenth Sunday after Pentecost* (Lutheran Worship).

the cloud was moving away from the tent, there—Miriam was scaly, like snow." "It is possible to retrieve Number's non-Priestly record using source criticism. The JE material begins in in Numbers 10:29 – 12:12… Numbers 11 (compare Exodus 16-18) recounts challenges to Moses' leadership role." The context church will be The Miracle Center of Faith Missionary Baptist Church. There are issues or complaints stemming from the Associate Ministers that affect the Pastor's leadership role. Katharine Doob Sakenfeld states, "Numbers 12:1-10, further confirms Moses' exclusive intimacy with Yahweh…"

According to Sakenfeld,

> Numbers 12:1-10 further confirms Moses' exclusive intimacy with Yahweh by recounting how Moses' siblings, Aaron and Miriam, criticized Moses for marrying a Cushite woman (compare Exodus 18:2, 6, 27). Yahweh summoned them to the tent of meeting, where he clearly defined Moses' unique charismatic status as a member of Yahweh's household, a human who beholds him face to face. As punishment, Miriam was afflicted by a pernicious skin ailment that is remitted because of Moses' entreaty.

New Testament Foundation

The New Testament continues the awareness of leadership through Jesus. When Jesus washed the Disciples feet, he demonstrated that as a Master, he could still serve. John 13:14, "If I then, your Lord and Master, have washed your feet, ye also ought to wash one another's feet." Many times, Pastors delegate out to other leaders to take care of the needs of the congregation. Fortunately, The Miracle Center of Faith Missionary Baptist Church has a Pastor that does lead and serve the people. Along with the Pastor, the First Lady, and the Associate Ministers have performed foot washing services during the Easter season. Foot washing is a humbling ceremony, but it demonstrates love and service to people who come together.

John 13:3-17 New International Version

³Jesus knew that the Father had put all things under his power, and that he had come from God and was returning to God; ⁴ so he got up from the meal, took off his outer clothing, and wrapped a towel around his waist. ⁵ After that, he poured water into a basin and began to wash his disciples' feet, drying them with the towel that was wrapped around him. ⁶ He came to Simon Peter, who said to him, "Lord, are you going to wash my feet?" ⁷ Jesus replied, "You do not realize now what I am doing, but later you will understand." ⁸ "No," said Peter, "you shall never wash my feet." Jesus answered, "Unless I wash you, you have no part with me." Then, Lord," Simon Peter replied, "not just my feet but my hands and my head as well!" ¹⁰ Jesus answered, "Those who have had a bath need only to wash their feet; their whole body is clean. And you are clean, though not every one of you." ¹¹ For he knew who was going to betray him, and that was why he said not every one was clean. ¹² When he had finished washing their feet, he put on his clothes and returned to his place. "Do you understand what I have done for you?" he asked them. ¹³ "You call me 'Teacher' and 'Lord,' and rightly so, for that is what I am. ¹⁴ Now that I, your Lord and Teacher, have washed your feet, you also should wash one another's feet. ¹⁵ I have set you an example that you should do as I have done for you. ¹⁶ Very truly I tell you, no servant is greater than his master, nor is a messenger greater than the one who sent him. ¹⁷ Now that you know these things, you will be blessed if you do them.[52]

Contextual Analysis

According to Grant R. Osborne, the opening verse of chapter 13 sets the scene for the whole of chapters 13--17. *Love* is one of the key terms in chapters 13--17, occurring thirty-one times in these five chapters as compared to only six times in chapters 1--12. Jesus now shows his disciples *the full extent [eis telos] of his love. Full extent*

---

[52] Holy Bible, *New International Version, NIV* (Colorado Springs, CO: Biblica, Inc.), 1973.

could also be translated *to the last* (cf. NIV note). The ambiguity is probably intentional, for the two meanings are related. Love is the laying down of one's life, and therefore to love completely means to love to the end of one's life (cf. 1 Jn 3:16). The love that has been evident throughout continues right up to the end. At the end, in the crucifixion, we will see the ultimate revelation of that love, that is, its *full extent.* This is now the third or fourth Passover mentioned (2:13; 6:4; perhaps 5:1). The shadow of the cross has been evident from the very outset through the references to Jesus' hour *(hora).* Jesus now knows that his hour has arrived (translated *time* in the NIV). John emphasizes the context of the Passover, for the lamb is about to be sacrificed for the sins of the world (1:29). That is part of the story, but it is also the occasion for Jesus to pass over *(metabe;* NIV, *leave)* from this world to the Father.[53]

For deeper discussion, H. R. Reynolds explains in verse 7, "In this verse every sentence is a distinct picture. He riseth from the supper, and layeth down his upper garments, and when he had taken a towel, he grided himself, then he poureth water into the washing basin. And he began to wash the feet of the disciples, and to wipe them with the towel wherewith he was girded."[54] Also, Don Fleming states,

When they gathered for the meal that night, Jesus took the place of a servant and washed the disciples' feet. By this action he symbolized firstly, the need for humility and secondly, that he, the perfect servant, would cleanse people from sin through his death (John 13:1-5). Peter, not understanding this symbolic action, objected. Jesus responded that if he refused to let Jesus cleanse him, he could not be Jesus' disciple. By this cleansing, Jesus was referring to cleansing from sin, something that Peter would understand more fully after Jesus had died, risen and been glorified (John 13:6-8; cf. Acts 5:30-31; 1 Peter 1:18-21; 2-24).[55]

---

[53]Grant R. Osborne, D. Stuart Briscoe, Haddon Robinson, IVP, 20 Vol *New Testament Commentaries* (Westmont, ILL: Inter Varsity Press), 2012, 151-190.

[54] H. R. Reynolds, *The Gospel of St. John Introduction and Exposition* (Grand Rapids, MI: WM. B. Eerdmans Publishing Co., 1978), 187.

[55]Don Fleming, *Concise BIBLE COMMENTARY* (Chattanooga, TN: AMG Publishers, 1988), 69.

Before Jesus was crucified, he told the Disciples there was a greater Commandment. He let them know that the greatest Commandment is "to love one another," John 13:34, "A new commandment I give unto you, that ye love one another; as I have loved you, that ye also love one another." Jesus let them know that by loving one another, people would know that he or she is a disciple for him. In this meaning, one can know that the person is a follower of Jesus Christ. H. R. Reynolds further explain verse 34, "The interpretation of this verse largely depends on the meaning given to the manner and type of love to you; then an amply sufficient explanation arises of the novelty of it."[56] The Associate Ministers should always be available to support the Pastor, assist other leaders, and serve in addressing the needs of the congregation. When Jesus washed the Disciples feet, Peter did not understand. However, Jesus did show all of them that he could be a leader/Master and still be a servant of God. Therefore, as a servant of God, the Associate Ministers should be motivated to serve with a smile. The Pastor has spoken or preached a sermon to help motivate the Associate Ministers, along with other leaders to lead and serve to create an atmosphere of showing love. For example, the Pastor will state, "Do not be like a wagon, because it must be pushed or pulled." Secondly, "Don't just show up when you want to," "Can you be found?" and "Don't make excuses."[57] As Associate Ministers, the Pastor expect them to pay their tithe and offerings, pray, witness for Jesus, and be evangelist persons, bringing the lost to know Christ. When these duties are performed one can see that support to the Pastor is primary and preaching becomes secondary. When the Associate Ministers begin to grasp this concept, they will become motivated and have a passion to lead a Ministry. Upon being motivated and leading a Ministry, they will become known for their service and preaching will fall in line in the context Church and outside in the community.

---

[56]Don Fleming, *Concise BIBLE COMMENTARY*, 196.
[57]Michael C. Turner, Dr., *The Miracle Center of Faith Missionary Baptist Church* (Capitol Heights, MD), 1991.

Detailed Analysis

According to Daniel B. Wallace, the author of John was the Apostle John. He is exact in mentioning names of characters in the book. Yet Wallace states, "If he is so careful, why does he omit the name of John unless he is John? Further, his mention of John the Baptist merely as "John"[58] (1:6) implies that if he is to show up in the narrative another name must be given him—such as "the beloved disciple"—or else confusion would result." Wallace concludes, "In conclusion, although John's Gospel is, as one author put it, "a maverick gospel," the traditional view of Johannine authorship is still the most reasonable hypothesis."[59] "In the standard order of the canonical gospels, John is fourth, after the three interrelated synoptic gospels Matthew, Mark and Luke."[60]

The literary context, the place of the Book of John is the fourth of the canonical gospels. D. A. Carson states, "The day of full-length treatments of John's gospel has come to a pause: there is no recent English competitor to Brown, Lindars. Morris, Schnackenburg (all three volumes now available in English), Barrett and Buitmann, nor one just over the horizon. Nevertheless, five developments deserve mention. Pride of place goes to the publication of the second edition of Barrett's justly famous commentary. Relatively little from the 1955 edition was *changed,* but about 100 pages of new material were added. In Barrett's own words, this commentary will seem to many to be 0ld-fashioned;9 but in certain respects that makes the work more valuable, not less. Whatever a reader may make of Barrett's stance on historical matters (fairly radical - *e.g.* 'I do not believe that John intended to supply us with historically verifiable information regarding the life and teaching of Jesus, and that historical traditions of great worth can be disentangled from his interpretative comments' IO), source critical

---

[58]Daniel B. Wallace, *Access dated May 2014, New Testament Studies, dts.edu,* (Dallas, TX, 2014).

[59]Daniel B. Wallace, *Access dated May 2014, New Testament Studies, dts.edu.*

[60]Daniel B. Wallace, *Access dated May 2014, New Testament Studies, dts.edu.*

questions (very conservative) or assessment of provenance (not a Palestinian work and not to be interpreted by Qumran), this commentary should take top billing for careful exegesis of the Greek text and for sane theological comment."[61]

For discussion, Ray Comfort presents, John 13, New Testament, History, Grace, supposedly written by John. The literary genre and structure of the book of John, is discussed by record. "The book of St. John is made up of several different types of literatures. There are laws, history accounts, prayers, prophecy, wilderness scenarios, and more. In large measure, however, the book may be described, similarly to Exodus and Leviticus, as law embedded in a narrative of theological history."[62]

Under the Hebrew Scriptures, Wallace continues to express as the major themes are, "At issue is whether the audience is principally believers or non-believers, whether this gospel is principally evangelistic or confirmatory. Although my own text-critical preference is for the present tense, not much should be made of this either way. Further, even if this document is seen as principally evangelistic, by analogy, would this suggest that the Roman congregation which Paul addresses is also principally unbelievers, on the basis of his statement in 1:15 (as well as the content of the whole book)?! Thus, the purpose of the book is to confirm or strengthen Gentile believers in their faith."[63] In addition, Wallace reported, "John not only wanted to make the literary connection with Paul's churches that Peter had done—he went the extra mile and took up residence in Ephesus himself. As we stated in our preface, the Gentile mission and the Gentiles' missionary are what drive the literary endeavors of the NT writers. John has certainly put his stamp of approval on Paul's gospel and efforts!"[64]

J. D. Douglas and Merrill C. Tenney does an overview of Numbers, stating, "The Author is anonymous, but comments else in

---

[61]D. A. Carson, Douglas J. Moo. *An introduction to the New Testament.* (Grand Rapids, MI: Zondervan, 2 New edition.), 2005, 233.

[62]Ray Comfort, *The Evidence Bible, NKJV* Nubian mercenaries belief (Alachua, FL: Bridge-Logos), 2012, 60-81.

[63]Daniel B. Wallace, *Access dated May 2014, New Testament Studies,dts.edu.*

[64]Daniel B. Wallace, *Access dated May 2014, New Testament Studies,dts.edu.*

the Bible seem to support the traditional view that Moses is responsible for the Pentateuch as a whole."[65] The spirit or passion to serve should be shown, even when a person is moving around throughout the world. If the Associate Ministers practice serving, it will become natural and not a chore. As Jesus moved from place to place, he had a compassionate heart. He went about, healing, serving, and doing good among the people. Associate Ministers should follow the pattern of Jesus to at least pray for those that need to be healed, serve people, and do good among the people. When Jesus was born the Angels declared, "Glory to God in the highest, and on earth, peace, goodwill toward men." Luke: 2:14. It certainly will be a grand time when there is peace on earth and goodwill toward men. The Associate Ministers should work along with the Pastor to help this world live in peace, show love, and create good will toward men and women.

The leader should have a vision. He or she should have a statement for the group, team, congregation, etc., to strive for. For example, to develop a cultural group of mutual respect for each other while working together. Each person should strive for excellence through whatever involvement is dealt with. Secondly, the leader should have a mission statement to spend time developing the ideals that are visualized. For example, the mission statement should let persons know what is being developed and how to accomplish the goals. The mission statement should let followers know how they can be part of the vision and plans that are put in place. The group, team, congregation, community, etc., will be dependable, respect each other, and complete the tasks set before them. The Miracle Center of Faith Missionary Baptist Church uses the mission statement as follows: "The mission of The Miracle Center of Faith Missionary Baptist Church is to exalt the Lord Jesus Christ and to spread the gospel at home and abroad. It is through the empowerment of believers through prayer, worship, education and the proclamation of the Gospel that we become transforming agents in a fragmented and dislocated world."

---

[65]J. D. Douglas, Merrill C. Tenney, *Zondervan Illustrated Bible Dictionary* (Grand Rapids, MI: Zondervan), 1987, 1029-1031.

In the project, the effort is to motivate the associate minister to have a positive attitude, have respect and "be responsible in their role."[66] In having a positive attitude, the associate ministers should display social skills that will not come back to the Pastor or congregation as a disgrace. He or she should be known as a willing worker with a positive manner. There are situations at The Miracle Center of Faith Missionary Baptist Church that have negative consequences. The pastor always has a vision or visions that are expressed to the leaders first and then brought to the congregation for consideration. There are times when everyone does not agree, but are peaceful, when displaying or expressing, their disagreements. It's possible, that there are others feeling the same expression, but have not expressed the comment. When people leave the church, one does not always know why the person or persons left. For example, persons, such as, the associate ministers should be in agreement with the pastor. When a disagreement occurs, it should be stated as afore mentioned, peacefully. However, this is not always, possible. There was a situation that could not be peacefully resolved. In the event, where the disagreement cannot be resolved, the associate minister usually, will leave the church. When the associate minister remains in the church, the person's attitude is usually, negative. This follower to the Pastor, yet leader of the congregation, is a reason for damaged fellowship and affects the unity of the whole church. These observed situations that exist and therefore, the Biblical Foundation, citing Moses, as the leader, Aaron, and Miriam as the followers is, "appropriate to establish the ideal the leaders and followers need to share the same vision."[67] Like Moses, Aaron, and Miriam, The Miracle Center of Faith Missionary Baptist Church had a pastor that spoke out to the other chosen leaders to form a church. Approximately 22 years ago, 12 founders stepped out on faith to establish the branch of Zion currently known as The Miracle Center of Faith Missionary Baptist Church. In

---

[66] K. Edward Copeland *Riding in the Second Chariot:* (Rockford, IL: Prayer Closet Publishing), 2004, 11-51.

[67] Theodore P. Fields, *All the Pastor's Men: The Associate Minister in the Black Church Setting* (Bloomington, IN: Authorhouse), 2002, 12-44.

an interview with the Pastor, these words were spoken, "God places ordinary people where He can use them as instruments of His will. Some of our founders have gone on to be with our Savior and we believe that they are still watching over us today. Others continue their work elsewhere, yet they continue to pray for the forward progression of Faith. Three of the original founders who are still with The Miracle Center, today are Reverend E. T. T., Deaconess P. M., and the precious "Holy Ghost."

When accepting or seeking a leadership position, does a leader consider the responsibility that is required? There are expectations that followers have or expect from the leader. The leader must set rules and regulations that people need. The leader is responsible for the decisions that are made and paths that are followed for success. In leading the way, the leader must set an example. The leader must first respect himself or herself and others. "The leader must know business to make sure all functions fall in place."[68] The leader must be a person with a positive attitude. In dealing with people around him or her, one must be able to give criticism, whether positive or negative to others. The Leader must receive the reaction of those that work with and around him or her. Imagine the awesome responsibilities that lie on the shoulder of President Obama. For example how does he really feel about the way the Republican portion of Congress react to his ideals and bills that need to be passed? Even, President Obama must adhere to certain rules, policies, and procedures. Thank goodness for the rules, policies and procedures that has been set for all persons to follow. The quote: "Hold yourself responsible for a higher standard than anybody expects of you. Never excuse yourself."— Henry Ward Beecher.

John C. Maxwell gives principles to focus on, such as, "attitude, influence, integrity, problem-solving, self-discipline, to name a few that have been discussed throughout this biblical foundation."[69]

---

[68]Carl F. Bird George, *Prepare Your Church for the Future:* (Grand Rapids, MI: Fleming H. Revell/Baker Books), 1992, 11-31.

[69] John C. Maxwell, *The 21 Irrefutable Laws of Leadership: Follow Them and People Will Follow You,* (Nashville, TN: Thomas Nelson, Inc.), 1998.

Maxwell adds, "when you recognize your lack of skill and begin the daily discipline of personal growth, exciting things start to happen. You start becoming an effective leader but you have to think about every move you make."[70]

Reflection

One should have influences from the natural world and spiritual world to have a full view of dealing with people. Also, life experiences will develop the principles that are mentioned to become a seasoned leader. In this world there are persons that want to live outside of the rules, policies, and procedures. Yes, these persons must be identified and dealt with. When average or below average is not good enough to remain on the team or in the organizations, what can the leader do? The leader must address the issues that affect the mass or majority of people. If a leader is not strong, he or she will sometimes let the issues grow worse. When the issue is not addressed, others aware will become discouraged. The Pastor/ Preacher as the leader of a congregation must address issues before they become concerns to the overall body of believers. Church is the place where the most misfits are tolerated. There was a young man who made a statement, "Only misfits go to church." In the ideal that, "all have a place" and "Live and let live" the Church society, constantly lower their standards. They maintain an air that all have a right to belong to the family of God. On the other hand, the secular world set standards that leave persons out.

There are leaders who abuse the power and authority that they possess. When a Leader is in a position of authority, it should be understood that the leader, will be fair. Thank goodness, there are guidelines in place to help all persons enjoy equality. Should one believes that the Bible is the, first guidance for principles of life to follow? If this is so, then those that are not believers will not have certain principles of life. The world law stands for those persons that "can or will suffer discrimination, need interpretation of law, politics,

---

[70]John C. Maxwell, *The 21 Irrefutable Laws of Leadership: Follow Them and People Will Follow You.*

and legal decisions."[71] In support of the proposed project, there are assumptions that are explored or investigated to bring the Biblical foundation to certain conclusions. For example, from the book, *"The Religions Book, Big Ideas Simply Explained."* the statement, " more than three quarters of the population consider themselves to hold some form of religious belief. Religion would seem to be a necessary part of human existence, as important to life as the ability to use language. Whether it is a matter of intense personal experience--an inner awareness of the divine--or a way of finding significance and meaning and providing a starting point for all of life's endeavors, it appears to be fundamental at a personal as well as a social level."[72]

Looking back at Genesis 6, one can read that God knew that man's heart was wicked. Genesis 6: 5, "And God saw that the wickedness of man was great in the earth, and that every imagination of the thoughts of his heart was only evil continually." In the midst of all that was going on, God decided to destroy the world, by flooding it. Noah and is family found favor with God, so they were saved. God had a plan to save Noah and his family, along with two of every, type of animal. These animals were male and female, in order, to reproduce, more animals. Just like the animals, male and female humans are meant to reproduce. However, look at the situations today, male and male plus female and female want to be together. These conditions are changing what was meant to be.

Further, people are cruel to one another, whereas, Jesus wanted people to love one another. There is so much cruelty being expressed that the "eye for an eye" punishment is being considered. It has come to a point that maybe, the type of punishment should be granted. For example, shooting someone should be punished by being shot. Perhaps, persons will think before a crime is committed.

In the midst of this world today, can we find trustworthiness, respect, fairness, responsibility, caring, and etc., to keep some sign of

---

[71]John W. Creswell, *Research Design, Qualitative & Quantitative Approaches:* (Thousand Oaks, CA: Sage Publications, Inc.), 1994, 1-20, 90-121.
[72]David Bland and Paul Reid. *The Religions Book: Big Ideas Simply Explained* (New York,, NY: COBALT ID. DK Publishing), 2003,42-69.

the compassion that Jesus exhibited? Has God and Jesus become a stranger to young people today? Certainly, the Holy Ghost or Holy Spirit is unknown and unspoken of by many young people. Have parents become ashamed to talk of, or call on the name of Jesus? If so, then this could be the reason Associate Ministers are not equipped with the proper backgrounds from parents. Perhaps, the positive steps or ways that are listed will help the Associate Ministers become motivated to a higher level. For example, (1) Accepting the Call from God to ministry, (2) Self-esteem, (3) Self-empowerment, along with empowerment from the Pastor, (4) Respecting others, and (5) Evaluating choices. When the Associate Ministers receive the Call to Ministry from God, they should be ready to accept the call and do the will of God. God's will is written as the Word of God should be read, obeyed, and carried out for the good of all. Primarily, self-esteem will come from within the spirit of a person. Along with respecting others, a person with some type of experience from youth will begin the process of respect. The scripture, Proverbs 22:6, "Train up a child in the way he should go and when he is old, he will not depart from it" is a principle that should be followed. Some grown up/adults did not receive the training required to satisfy the Proverbs saying. Therefore, young teenagers acquire the same pattern and usually get in trouble with school or law authorities. In cases, like these, mentors and voices of authority, are required to help shape persons to fit in the normal pattern of society. When persons are taught to respect themselves, then it is usually spread to respecting others. There is always hope that a person will change for the better. There are Associate Ministers that have become discouraged with life, but still hold on to the position. They have failed in certain areas and have forgotten that God will give second chances and forgives us for sins. These persons can become new creatures, similar to being baptized, and help others that are lost in the world. When motivated to go forward, not just trying to preach when assigned, but accepting a ministry or starting a ministry, much can be accomplished.

    Does Preaching and Leadership overlap or complement each other? When a leader commits himself or herself to a position of leadership, what are the guidelines that he or she should follow? We live in a society of moral ethics. Each person is responsible for his or her actions. When religiously based, one may say the Golden Rule, "Do unto others as you would have them do unto you." However, from the moral values, of the world, one would say, "treat others the way you want to be treated." Are we not saying the same thing in reality? Everyone wants to feel that he or she is treated fairly.

The Preacher should be a leader or at least have leadership characteristics. For example, the prophet Timothy had to be encouraged by Paul to be strong. The background of his grandmother, Lois, and his mother, Eunice, had to be brought to his remembrance to remind him of strength. In order for Timothy to finally speak out and be strong, he had to become strong. In reference to Timothy gaining strength, the scripture, 2 Timothy 2:7, "Consider what I say and the Lord give thee understanding in all things" can be used. This scripture shows that Timothy had gained strength in his preaching, writing and knew that confirmation could be found through the Lord.

Both a Preacher and a Leader need protection from evil. Jesus alerted the Disciples that Satan had come to "kill, steal, and destroy." However, he came that they may have life, and have it more abundantly." [73] Just like Timothy required boldness in sharing the gospel, preachers need boldness. Also, the leader needs boldness in making and holding a group or team together. Preachers and their Leaders need unity among the church/congregation. Leaders need unity among the group or team. Then, like Solomon, asked for wisdom, the Preachers and Leaders need wisdom and understanding from God. In order to influence others, one need God's grace, and must have gift(s) from God. What is the gift that is given to a person to lead and influence others? As one take time out to read scriptures from chapter 12 of Romans, it is written that there are "gifts differing according to the grace that is given to us."

In summary, this Biblical Foundation should give the Associate Ministers or any reader understanding of the method to do biblical interpretation. By using the textbook, *A Road Map*, by Fred Tiffany and Sharon Ringe, one will have the guidelines to complete a task for interpretation. Old Testament and New Testament scriptures have been presented and interpreted to further prepare a biblical foundation for the upcoming project. With a focus on Preaching and Leadership in the Black Church, the Biblical Foundation content should help the Associate Ministers become motivated to perform to a much higher level in ministry. With the understanding of the Bible, the Associate Ministers should be prepared to preach at any time. However, when

---

[73] John 10:10, *NIV*.

the opportunity is not given, they should engage in perfecting the ministry and other support and serving opportunities that has been assigned to them. This will be discussed farther in the proposed project.

CHAPTER THREE

THEOLOGICAL FOUNDATIONS

The purpose of this writing is to bring clarity to the Theological Foundation for the course or focus on Preaching and Leadership in the Black Church. Based on the proposed project dealing with the motivation of the Associate Ministers, the Theological Foundation will be a benefit to those interested in religion in support of the Pastor. Walter J. Chantry's, small, book, *Today's Gospel authentic or synthetic?*, will make one sit up and take notice of the theology that we define for the public. His review of the Evangelicals, for example, "Evangelicals cherish their Reformation heritage. We stand in the line of Luther and others who have broken the back of Papal superstitions. The Bible, God's Holy Word, is our guide in all things. We bow to no human authority."[1]

Throughout the Introduction, Chantry let's one know that the "evangelical wing of the Protestant church is saturated with doctrine and practices which have no Biblical foundation."[2] Further, Chantry writes that "we have inherited a system of evangelistic preaching which is unbiblical."[3] He believes the teachings "cannot be traced to the Scriptures."[4]

Also, he states, "They, the messages, have clearly arisen from superficial exegesis and a careless mixture of twentieth-century reason with God's revelation."[5]

Chantry would want Preachers to give careful attention to the Gospel of God's Word alone. In dealing with the Theology Foundation, one must be careful to present God's Word. Chantry, went

---

[1] Walter J. Chantry, *Today's Gospel authentic or synthetic? The Banner of Trust* (Edinburgh, UK: 1970, East Peoria, IL: Versa Press, Inc.), 2006, 3, 32-51.
[2] Walter J. Chantry, *Today's Gospel authentic or synthetic.*
[3] Walter J. Chantry, *Today's Gospel authentic or synthetic.*
[4] Walter J. Chantry, *Today's Gospel authentic or synthetic.*
[5] Walter J. Chantry, *Today's Gospel authentic or synthetic.*

on to say, "When a half truth is presented as the whole truth, it becomes an untruth."⁶ One must as Chantry writes, "take a firm stand on the content of the Gospel…tell the story…be precisely Jesus' story…"⁷ Finally, as Chantry would, write, "Learn to follow the Christ of the Scriptures in evangelism. Lay hold of the authentic Gospel and discard the synthetic."⁸

Chantry's writing will give one the guideline to glorify God. He used the rich young ruler as an example to show how Jesus received the young ruler and taught him about how to receive eternal life. When the "rich" young ruler addressed him, as, "Good Master," Jesus, informed him that there were none good, except his Father in heaven. "It is God alone who is originally and essentially good."⁹ Chantry continues to bring to light that Jesus "chief aim in every act was to do the will of His Father and to make His glory known to men."¹⁰ Further, Chantry makes it known that Jesus wanted God to be glorified. For example, Chantry wrote, "Upon humbling Himself to enter this world Christ said, Lo, "I come to do thy will, O God" [Hebrews 10:7]. In life He reported, "I do always those things that please him" [John 8:29]. As He went to the cross, Jesus summarized His ministry thus: "I have glorified thee on the earth: I have finished the work which thou gavest me to do" [John 17:4]. This burning passion consumed Him throughout his life."¹¹

Another source defines theology this way:
> The word "theology" comes from two Greek words that combined mean "the study of God." Christian theology is simply an attempt to understand God as He is revealed in the Bible. No theology will ever fully explain God and His ways because God is infinitely and eternally higher than we

---

⁶Walter J. Chantry, *Today's Gospel authentic or synthetic? The Banner of Trust* (Edinburgh, UK: 1970, East Peoria, IL: Versa Press, Inc.), 2006, 51-70.

⁷Walter J. Chantry, *Today's Gospel authentic or synthetic? The Banner of Trust.*

⁸Walter J. Chantry, *Today's Gospel authentic or synthetic? The Banner of Trust.*

⁹Walter J. Chantry, *Today's Gospel authentic or synthetic? The Banner of Trust.*

¹⁰Walter J. Chantry, *Today's Gospel authentic or synthetic? The Banner of Trust, 51-70.*

¹¹Walter J. Chantry, *Today's Gospel authentic or synthetic? The Banner of Trust.*

are. Therefore, any attempt to describe Him will fall short (Romans 11:33-36). However, God does want us to know Him insofar as we are able, and theology is the art and science of knowing what we can know and understand about God in an organized and understandable manner. Some people try to avoid theology because they believe it is divisive. Properly understood, though, theology is uniting. Proper, biblical theology is a good thing; it is the teaching of God's Word (2 Timothy 3:16-17). The study of theology, then, is nothing more than digging into God's Word to discover what He has revealed about Himself. When we do this, we come to know Him as Creator of all things, Sustainer of all things, and Judge of all things. He is the Alpha and Omega, the beginning and end of all things. When Moses asked who was sending him to Pharaoh, God replied "I AM WHO I AM" (Exodus 3:14). The name I AM indicates personality. God has a name, even as He has given names to others. The name I AM stands for a free, purposeful, self-sufficient personality. God is not an ethereal force or a cosmic energy. He is the almighty, self-existing, self-determining Being with a mind and a will—the "personal" God who has revealed Himself to humanity through His Word, and through His Son, Jesus Christ.[12]

In telling the Jesus story, one can use the Scripture, John 8:32. "If you abide in my Word you are my disciple indeed." One must know that there are manmade doctrines in Churches, but the Bible is or should be used as the True Word of God. Therefore, Jesus spoke in John 7:17, "If anyone wills to do God's will, he shall know concerning the doctrine, whether it is from God…"

Throughout history it has been shown that man is not totally satisfied with his religion. From the beginning of time, sin creped in

---

[12] *What is Theology, access date July 2014, Read more:* http://www.gotquestions.org/what-is-theology.html#ixzz34vtnOZfX

from Satan through Eve, in the Garden of Eden. This began as documented in the first book of the Bible, the chapter called Genesis. Surprisingly, by chapter 6 of Genesis, God noted that man's heart was sinful and he was sorry that he had created man. Further, God decided to allow a flood to come and destroy man, except for Noah and his family. Based on this religious story, one can see that man has been in a battle with his flesh and spirit since the beginning of time. According to Chantry, "The Holy Spirit has come to lead the sincere disciple of Jesus into "all truth."[13] "Real Scriptural truth can only be found in the light of the entire context of Scripture."[14]

According to Jon Macquarrie, "Christian theology seeks to think the Church's faith as a coherent whole. It aims not only at showing the internal coherence of the Christian faith, that is to say, how the several doctrines constitute a unity, but also at exhibiting the coherence of this faith with the many other beliefs and attitudes to which we are committed in the modern world. Only if these tasks are accomplished can the faith be held intelligently and be integrated with the whole range of human life."[15] When Christian doctrines are used or presented to the Church as a whole, those assembled together become more like minded. When books and documents are used persons can use them as reference and easily discuss or express proven methods. The context, The Miracle Center of Faith Missionary Baptist Church is known for its Miracle Center Academy. There are persons who attend that are not members of the Church, but like being in the classes that are taught. The Pastor has a heart for people and will open the doors of the Church to interested persons. By including persons of different backgrounds and even different religions, a varied perspective is brought out that will address the differences in the world and how to deal theologically will different races, cultures, and even those who do not want to believe they have religious beliefs.

---

[13] Walter J. Chantry, *Today's Gospel authentic or synthetic? The Banner of Trust* (Edinburgh, UK: 1970, East Peoria, IL: Versa Press, Inc.), 2006, 51-70.

[14] Walter J. Chantry, *Today's Gospel authentic or synthetic? The Banner of Trust.*

[15] John Macquarrie, *Principles of Christian Theology.* Second Edition. (New York, NY: Charles Scribner's Sons.), 1977, 1-12, 35-48.

Further, Macquarrie, states, "The theological task needs to be done over and over again, as new problems, new situations, and new knowledge comes along. But there are many pitfalls along the way. Sometimes the theologian gets lost in academic speculations that are far removed from the living faith of the Church; sometimes he clings tenaciously to the myths and symbols of a bygone age; sometimes in a pathetic desire to be "contemporary" and "relevant," he reduces the Christian faith to a pale reflection of whatever happens to be the currently popular philosophy. No theologians can hope to avoid all the pitfalls."[16]

McGreal's book, "Great Thinkers of the Western World" was primarily used for the Theoretical Foundation. However, due to certain theological thoughts, this book is used as a reference for Theological thoughts. For example, the first writer to be presented was Parmenides, who had thoughts of the "one god… [who]… abides in the selfsame place, moving not at all" and who is identical with the whole world."[17] McGreal wrote that "Parmenides, it is quite clear that his thought makes a watershed in pre-Socratic philosophy. Parmenide's thoughts coming at the close of the sixth century, B.C., was influenced by both the worldly, scientific, and cosmological views of early Greek philosophical inquiry and the Orphic religions revival of the sixth century, with the focus on ecstasy, the reality of the soul as divine, the ultimate reality of the "One God who dwells in all."[18]

Life will show that every theologian will face certain pitfalls, as mentioned. However, there is hope, because Macquarrie, states, "Yet the fact that every theologian will have some flaws it is not a reason for turning away from the theological task or for underestimating the place of theology in the Church's life… It is foolish, for instance, to suggest that we need devote ourselves only to Church by such sciences

---

[16]John Macquarrie, *Principles of Christian Theology*.

[17]Ian P. McGreal, *Great Thinkers of the Western World*. (New York, NY: Harper Resource, Harper Collins Publishers), 1992, 1-16, 25-49, 115-171.

[18]Ian P. McGreal, *Great Thinkers of the Western World*.

as psychology and sociology… Every theologian must write from his own perspective, and this will be limited in various ways."[19]

When discussions are raised about religion, one will find that depending on a persons' religious background through parents, Church, and outside influences, beliefs will be different. For example, the Jehovah Witness, Catholic, Muslim, Seven Day Adventist, and Baptist will raise strong arguments against and among each other, believing that each religion, in its own way, is the correct way. However, Baptist appears to be stronger through the belief of the King James Version of the Bible that Jesus Christ is the "way", based on John 14:6, Jesus said, "I am the way, the truth, and the life, no man cometh to the father, but by me." This quote has quieted many argues that could go on for hours, days, and over time.

As theology evolves through time, one is still, yet, drawn to world scholars, such as Sigmund Freud. The quote from him, "If I cannot move the heavens I will stir up the internal regions." [20] This quote was from an epigraph to the interpretation of dreams that the writer, Sharon Heller brought about through her writing of Sigmund Freud dealing with him from "A to Z." In reading the preface by Heller, in support of the project, one is drawn to the expression, "A century ago, Freud jolted the world, and it has never been the same. Love him or hate him, the inferences and reverberations of Freud's observations have irrevocable altered Western civilization."[21] Freud is known to have used "scientific tools" that crossed the bounds of psychology. Freud, using, "his insights, into the unconscious, gave us a language, to probe the uncharted territory of the human mind, changing how we conceptualize human nature."[22] Freud opened the door to reflect on "childhood experiences" to help mold our later emotional life, "our behavior has disguised motives, and "that dreams have symbolic meaning."[23] Heller writes that "Freud did not discover the unconscious

---

[19] John Macquarrie, *Principles of Christian Theology.* Second Edition. (New York, NY: Charles Scribner's Sons), 1977, 21-48.
[20] Sharon Heller, *Freud A to Z.* (Hoboken, N J: John Wiley & Sons, Inc.), 2005, 51-72, 97-112.
[21] Sharon Heller, *Freud A to Z.*
[22] Sharon Heller, *Freud A to Z.*

mind. Poets and philosophers, writers such as Goethe and Schiller, whom Freud frequently quoted, looked to the unconscious mind for the roots of creativity. Freud provided a roadmap to navigate our psychic life. "Psychoanalysis was forced, through the study of pathological repression," Freud observed, to "take the concept to the "unconscious" seriously"—to elucidate how our feelings, thoughts, fears, and actions are far more intricate and fascinating than they appear on the surface, as they emerge through our dreams, jokes, slips of the tongue, mistakes, and other actions."[24] Freud armed us "with a way to probe this heretofore inaccessible cavern of the mind, he gave us a way to alleviate human suffering."[25]

According to Grunlan and Mayers, "There is no study of man more encompassing than the study of anthropology… When an investigator enters the field and begins serious study, he discovers that man's past and present culture opens a vast panorama."[26]

In studying theology, it has been brought out that there is a contemporary theological movement, which involves Black theology and Liberation theology. These two stand out for the African-American, because during slavery, they were not even allowed to read or write. However, the African-American culture has added to the history of the religious and Christian theologians. For example, James H. Cone writes *"Liberation A Black Theology of Liberation"* book that maintains that the black race had a religion in Africa and brought their thoughts and ways with them. However, the white culture dominated the black culture, causing the black culture to accept new thoughts and ways. In the midst of the new ways, the Bible became for the black culture based on Cone's expression, "Christian theology is a theology of liberation."[27] Cone wrote that "The black man's religion is a critical

---

[23]Sharon Heller, *Freud A to Z.*

[24]Sharon Heller, *Freud A to Z.*

[25] Stephen A. Grunlan and Marvin K. Mayers, *Cultural Anthropology. A Christian Perspective.* (Grand Rapids, MI: Academie Books, Zondervan Publishing House), 1979, 1-21, 48-60.

[26]Stephen A. Grunlan and Marvin K. Mayers, *Cultural Anthropology. A Christian Perspective.*

[27]James H. Cone, *Liberation A Black Theology of Liberation* The C. Eric Series

component of his passage from slavery to a freedom which is still to be perfected."[28] Imagine, in 1970, Cone wanted white America to be aware of the religion of black America. In the Foreword, Cone expressed himself with these words, "This series is addressed to white America, too. The black experience—religious, social, economic, political—is writ large in the cultural development of the larger society. Understanding it is crucial to an informed perspective of what America is or can become."[29] Further, from research through ask.com, the liberation theology is defined as "a rational study in the being of God in the world in light of the existential situation of an oppressed community relating the forces of liberation to the essence of the Gospel which is Jesus Christ."[30]

"At a time when others make predictions about the future of our community and paint a gloomy picture of the extinction of African American people as a distinct entity, we need Black Theology. We need it because we must claim not only the faith of our mothers and fathers, but understand what we are up against today and the work we must do to claim our future."[31]

There are different types of theology. However, in this Doctoral study, the religion is the primary theology to create discussion. Based on the definition, religion is the human expression towards supernatural being, but theology is the study of God's nature.[32] Further, philosophy has come into the discussions as research is applied to find answers for the theology foundation. Therefore, the definition, "theology is the study of religion, philosophy is the investigation of the truths and principles of being, knowledge, or conduct."[33] Then it is good to know that there are different theologies

---

in Black Religion (Philadephia, PA:J. B. Lippincott Co.), 1970, 1-42, 60-78.
   [28]James H. Cone, *Liberation A Black Theology of Liberation.*
   [29]James H. Cone, *Liberation A Black Theology of Liberation.*
   [30] Ask.com, access dated May 2015.
   [31]Ask.com , access dated May 2015.
   [32]Stephen A. Grunlan and Marvin K. Mayers. *Cultural Anthropology. A Christian Perspective.* (Grand Rapids, MI: Academie Books. Zondervan Publishing House), 1979.
   [33]Stephen A. Grunlan and Marvin K. Mayers, *Cultural Anthropology. A Christian Perspective.*

of Christianity, i.e., Orthodox, Catholic, Lutheran, Methodist, Baptist, etc.

Since, the context is, The Miracle Center of Faith Missionary Baptist Church, it is necessary to find as much theology as possible to relate to the context. Further, the definition of Deity versus Divinity is helpful in this theology foundation. Therefore, "Deity refers to who God is; Divinity refers to having the attributes of God--what God does. Colossians 2:9 illustrates Christ's deity: For the entire fullness..."[34]

In support of the research, the following will help to explain Christian theology and give an "overview of the assigned course.: "Christian theology--enterprise to construct a coherent system of Christian belief and practice based primarily upon the texts of the Old Testament and the New Testament as well as the historic traditions of the faithful. Christian theologians use biblical exegesis, rational analysis, and argument to clarify, examine, understand, explicate, critique, defend or promote Christianity. Theology might be undertaken to help the theologian better understand Christian tenets."[35] make comparisons between Christianity and other traditions,[36] defend Christianity against objections and criticism, facilitate reforms in the Christian church, [37]assist in the propagation of Christianity, [38] draw on the resources of the Christian tradition to address some present situation or need,[39] or for a variety of other reasons.

Roland H. Bainton's book, *Christendom, A Short History of Christianity and Its Impact on western Civilization* does a good history of telling of how the Church had begun, but also how the Churches

---

[34]Stephen A. Grunlan and Marvin K. Mayers, *Cultural Anthropology. A Christian Perspective.*

[35]Stephen A. Grunlan and Marvin K. Mayers. *Cultural Anthropology. A Christian Perspective.*

[36]Stephen A. Grunlan and Marvin K. Mayers, *Cultural Anthropology. A Christian Perspective.*

[37]Stephen A. Grunlan and Marvin K. Mayers, *Cultural Anthropology. A Christian Perspective.*

[38]Stephen A. Grunlan and Marvin K. Mayers, *Cultural Anthropology. A Christian Perspective.*

[39]Roland H. Bainton, *Christendom, A Short History of Christianity and Its Impact on western Civilization* (Nashville, TN: Abington Press), 1966.

were dissolve and why. The following is an excerpt, "Menacing forces of dissolution in the Church during the late Middle Ages appeared to have been dispelled in the early years of the sixteenth century. Sectarianism and heresy had largely been crushed. Savonarola had been burned, leaving behind him no following. The conciliar movement had been subordinated to papal control, and the schism had been terminated. Spain, long torn between the crescent and the cross, was now definitely aligned with Christendom; the rigors of the Inquisition could be relaxed. As a consequence, Christendom enjoyed, in the first quarter of the century, a period of relative tranquility and liberalism. Yet there were unrest and dissatisfaction within the Church, and they were justified. Corruption in the Church was rampant, and rampant, and many high-minded churchmen throughout Europe bemoaned and derelictions and clamored for reform. Complaints centered on three points: immorality among the clergy, severe financial demands imposed upon the faithful, and neglect of the parishes."[40]

In the writing of the theological foundation, shall a person study God? In the research of theology, it can be said that "you can't study God, however you study the "word" of God that has been given through various people…" further, [41]"many people focus on certain aspects only because to study every word is a little overwhelming."[42]

The question can be raised, is a personal relationship the answer to knowing, studying, understanding, and even teaching theology? Through research it has been found that even an atheist can teach theology…the atheist has knowledge to read and study theology from a "liberal" point of view. In the meantime, it has been shown that the person or persons with thorough knowledge of the Bible and other theology can become to, well educated in interpretation that they begin

---

[40]Roland H. Bainton, CHRISTENDOM A Short History of Christianity and Its Impact on Western Civilization Vol. II From the Reformation to the Present (New York, NY: Harper Colophon Books Harper & Row, Publishers), 1966, 91-110.

[41]Roland H. Bainton, *CHRISTENDOM A Short History of Christianity and Its Impact on Western Civilization.*

[42]Roland H. Bainton, *CHRISTENDOM A Short History of Christianity and Its Impact on Western Civilization.*

to go beyond the written word of God. In this case, would a personal relationship with God control how far a person will take the interpretation of the Word of God?

When exegesis of the Word of God is done, how much of the world thought it should be projected to the congregation? For example: When a politician proclaim the Word of God, how much do the Christian gain from their interpretation? Thank goodness for those persons who from a Baptist perspective for clarification for the context Church, i.e., Millard Erickson, who was Academic Dean at Bethel Theological Seminary in St. Paul Minnesota. In 1985, his writing of Christian Theology gives a "clear and thorough" writing of systematic theology from a Baptist perspective. His writing is believed to be clear for dealing with "major trends in non-evangelical theology, and helpful for personal application." Erickson was last known as teaching in Southwestern Baptist Seminary at Fort Worth, Texas. Then, one is inclined to remember that we are in a Methodist atmosphere at the United Theological Seminary and therefore, should be aware of Methodist theology. For example, Thomas Oden in his writing, The Living God, Systematic Theology, Vol.1, he gives the early history of the church. In his early beliefs, it is said that he was "moved from his previous liberal theological convictions to a conservative evangelical position. This can lead one to believe that his or her convictions can be persuaded from liberal to conservative in the Baptist or Methodist realm. Further, research has shown that Augustus H. Strong, also, wrote about Systematic Theology. In his years, 1836-1921, as an adult, he was president and professor of theology in New York at the Rochester Theological Seminary. Also, he was the first president of the Northern Baptist Convention. His, Systematic Theology was "widely used in Baptist circles for most of the twentieth century, until it was largely replaced by Millard Erickson's Christian Theology (1983-85)." This is a prime example of how time and different views can change or expand beliefs.

CHAPTER FOUR

PROJECT ANALYSIS

This project analysis will attempt to show how the final project and final document results from the research and processes have been accomplished. The project, Solidifying the Relationship Between the Pastor and Associate Ministers examined the problem and sort solutions and steps to reach a conclusion. The model of ministry used a hypothesis regarding why the Associate Ministers only wanted to preach. Through solidifying or defining the roles of Associate Ministers to serve, hopefully the level of motivation would be raised.

Problem:

The Associate Ministers are not motivated to do anything, but preach. This low level of motivation by Associate Ministers is a concern for the context church, The Miracle Center of Faith Missionary Baptist Church. The Associate Ministers fail to advance to a high level of excellence while serving as Associate Ministers.

Purpose:

Support to the Pastor through serving is the primary duty. There is researching going on to seek to find new ways to develop new skills or new approaches to raise the levels of excellence. Further, continue, trying to find ways to solve problems that created the low levels of excellence for the Associate Ministers.

The methodology used for this project used the qualitative method. According to C. Pope and N. Mays, "Qualitative research is an umbrella term that covers a variety of styles of social research, drawing on a variety of disciplines such as sociology, anthropology, and psychology."[1] "The goal of qualitative research is the development

---

[1] C. Pope, N. Mays, *Qualitative Research: Rigour and qualitative research* (BMJ., 1995), 109-122.

of concepts which help us to understand social phenomena in natural (rather than experimental) settings, giving due emphasis to the meanings, experiences, and views of all participants."[2] The first data was collected through the form of questions. These questions, along with a survey generated responses.

Expected Results

The model of ministry designed by the qualitative method through questions surveys, interviews, case studies will assist to create steps to follow for other pastors. The solidifying of the relationship between the pastor and associate ministers will bring about an understanding of what God expect from a leader and the followers. This project will become an ongoing project or process that can be repeated by other churches or in the community. Upon the implementation of this project and desired results, it will be presented to the pastor, associate ministers, church as a teaching document and possibly published for the public.

The proposed project revealed as a stated problem that was perceived at The Miracle Center of Faith Missionary Baptist Church in Capitol Heights, Maryland. This Church has, at that time, eighteen persons named as Associate Ministers to the Pastor. The primary assignment is to serve the Pastor. Each Associate Minister has been assigned certain functions by the pastor to perform during his or her tenure at The Miracle Center Church. These functions include leading a church ministry, such as, Senior Ministry, Youth Ministry, Nursing Home, Homeless, Prison and Share Ministries.

The Associate Ministers find themselves wanting to preach, rather than serve in the assigned functions. Therefore, it has become apparent that there is a low level of motivation toward getting assignments done. It was necessary that a plan be designed to find out the self-interest and passion of each Associate Minister to create an atmosphere of service before being assigned to the Preaching

---

[2]C. Pope, N. Mays, *Qualitative Research: Rigour and qualitative research.*

Schedule. In order to achieve a satisfactory goal this Project Proposal was designed by a plan or model of ministry to identify how the Associate Ministers would participate. It is hoped that in the project and through research methods that have been tried and tested the Proposed Project will obtain certain results. These results include, but are not limited to, leading a church ministry that will satisfy each Associate Minister's self-interest and passion. In the meantime, Associate Ministers will become known for their assigned ministry and give much value to the congregation and community for their service.

Field Experience

Qualitative research method is the primary way for investigating the chosen topic of dealing with the motivation of the Associate Ministers. The data has been collected by questions, surveys, interviews, and observations. "This qualitative study is a phenomenological approach which includes a survey, interviews, and case studies, that focused on human experience."[3]

Interpretative Phenomenological Analysis (IPA) is an approach to psychological qualitative research with an idiographic focus, which means that it aims to offer insights into how a given person, in a given context, makes sense of a given phenomenon.[4]

Usually these phenomena relate to experiences of some personal significance - such as a major life event, or the development of an important relationship. The plan and execution of this study was used for over more than six months and continuously shows human experiences that took place based on the qualitative research method. From the time of proposing a project, there was a need to raise the level of motivation for the Associate Ministers in the context Church. Upon speaking with the Pastor of The Miracle Center of Faith Missionary Baptist Church in a meeting, the need was concurred by an

---

[3]Gill, M. J., *The Possibilities of Phenomenology for Organizational Research Methods, 17:2, 118-137.*

[4]Wikipedia, the free encyclopedia

agreement to begin the process. The purpose of this study was to investigate which ministries could satisfy the self-interest or passion of the Associate Ministers. This study would involve fifteen Associate Ministers. There are eighteen Associate Ministers, but three are exempt from the study, due to age, sickness, inactivity, or on assignment for other duties. Following the meeting, a plan was laid out to have scheduled meetings and to conduct a survey. The Survey consisted of eight questions about the Associate Minister's self-interest and passion for ministry. Also, the Associate Ministers had to write an essay about their experience with other Churches, their call to Ministry, and their expectations from this venture as Associate Minister. See Appendix A for a copy of the Steps that were followed after the "call to ministry." This is an excerpt, "Upon successful completion of the Trial Sermon, the person will be called, 'Minister' and welcomed as an Associate Minister to the Minister's Council to serve in the suggested Church Ministry as the lead, serve as support to the Pastor, and to the Congregation. Then Associate Minister is then ready for training by the Pastor, or other lead ordained Clergy, Reverends, and on to a University for further structured studies. The age, mind, and circumstances of the Associate Minister will determine what he or she is able to comprehend. As time pass, approximately, three month intervals, each Associate Minister will be evaluated for his or her advancement in the assigned Church Ministry, support to the Pastor, and support and service to the Congregation. If one is producing good results as a leader of the chosen Ministry, the Associate Minister will become known among the congregation and community. At this time, the Associate Minister will be called on for services, which may lead to a position as a Pastor or other advanced duties.

    Also, during the meeting, schedules were set to visit certain institutions, i.e., the Prince George's County Correction Center, the Prince George's County Hospital, The Addison Road Homeless Shelter, Prince George's County and Laurel Rehabilitation and Nursing Center, etc. The Prince George's County Correction Center has been the most active in coordinating with the Church to provide offenders for Community Service. Also, the Addison Road Homeless Shelter has provided services to women and children in need of food and temporary shelter. Whenever, a Church member experience a family crisis, research is quickly done to find ways to help.

The Project research weekly meetings were scheduled for at least eight weeks, since June 21, 2013, to October 30.2013, and remain presently scheduled on a monthly basis. The continuous meetings are labeled as the Minister's Council Meetings. Each Associate Minister was asked about their feelings. Each was asked about which Ministry appealed to him or her most for leadership and participation. The feelings of possible spiritual gifts from each leader, is important for making a choice of a Church ministry. The survey that was generated and presented to the Associate Ministers was viewed as an overall good presentation of data. The reactions were mixed, the results were gathered and each result was unique to the individual completing the survey. The Associate Ministers has some understanding that this study was taking place. Each person was interviewed in a one on one fashion with questions that would generate a somewhat expected result. It should be noted that the one-on-one sessions/interviews are considered as a Pre-Test. However, if a Pre-Test is required to be written out, it can be produced with certain information removed from the content. Also, the Profile Sheet is considered private, but certain information can be removed and provided if required. In regard to meetings, events, visits, details of incidents that occurred, and other observations, reports have been generated and discussed in meetings. In the end, it is hoped that results would occur that could be duplicated for other Pastors.

    The research of the qualitative research method explained that it consists of a number of differently developed methods that are best suited to address questions of particular interest. There are however, some general themes of qualitative research design that apply across all approaches and methodologies. "Qualitative research is an umbrella term that covers a variety of styles of social research, drawing on a variety of disciplines such as sociology, anthropology, and psychology."[5] "The goal of qualitative research is the development of concepts which help us to understand social phenomena in natural (rather than experimental) settings, giving due emphasis to the meanings, experiences, and views of all participants."[6] The first data was collected through the form of questions. These questions, along with a survey generated responses. Also, reactions have led to the steps that can be taken to raise the level of the motivation and potential within the Associate Ministers. The questions were generated to bring out self-interest and passion details that could show the proper fit for the Church ministries. From the responses or answers, it became apparent that several Associate Ministers are motivated to study farther to become qualified to be Pastors. There are others that have reached ages that only in house training will help and life time experience. There are at least three Associate Ministers that have reached the age of seventy years and do not plan to attend a college or university. As persons age, some use age as an excuse not to study. The excuse for being married, older, and sickness of mother, father, husband, or wife, can generate multiple reasons for lack of motivation. For example, some will only want to attend one of the two services on Sunday morning at 7:30 a.m. and 10:00 a.m. Then certainly, for the preaching engagements that occur for the Pastor at 3:30 p.m. the excuses have already been noted. Further, the Tuesday evening, 6:45 p.m. Bible Study and 7:30 p.m. Prayer and Praise it is just too much and too dark for them to attend. However, these are events that are considered as necessary for those serving in leadership roles. John W. Creswell in his method approaches express, "the researcher keeps a focus on learning the meaning that the participants hold about the problem or issue."[7] Also, Creswell defines phenomenological research as "a strategy of inquiry in which the researcher identifies the essence of human experiences about a phenomenon as described by

---

[5]C. Pope, N. Mays, *Qualitative Research: Rigour and qualitative research* (BMJ., 1995), 109-122.

[6]C. Pope, N. Mays, *Qualitative Research: Rigour and qualitative research.*

[7]John W. Creswell, *Research Design: Qualitative, Quantitative, and Mixed Method Approaches* (Thousand Oaks, CA: SAGE Publications, 2009), 175.

participants."⁸ Further, Creswell uses the qualitative observations where "the researcher takes field notes on the behavior and activities of individuals at the research site."⁹ I have observed the low self-esteem type behavior of the Associate Ministers and found that they needed something to occur to raise their level of motivation. During the Biblical Foundation writing and choice of Numbers 11 and Numbers 12, it was discovered that the characteristics of Aaron and Miriam were similar to the Associate Ministers. There was complaining, jealously, loss of interest, and movement made to appear impatient with Moses. In the review of Numbers 11 and 12, there are verses that give details of the Israelites' mannerism. These are also, apparent characteristics that existed at the context of interest, The Miracle Center of Faith Missionary Baptist Church. If Miriam and Aaron had followed the leadership of Moses as delegated, stayed within their roles, adhered to the following writing of Spurgeon, their situation would not exist:

Based on the writing of Spurgeon, as stated, "There is a clear analogy between the leadership of Moses for Israel and the leadership of a pastor among God's people. The analogy does not fit at every point, but in many aspects:

- o   God was recognized as the true leader of the people.
- o   The leader could not do the work of leadership alone.
- o   The leader had a special responsibility for prayer and teaching.
- o   The leader must select, train, and give authority to others to help in the work.
- o   The people had a definite role in all this (Deuteronomy 1:13)"¹⁰

Choose some wise, understanding and respected men from each of your tribes, and I will set them over you. It became a challenge to

---

⁸John W. Creswell, *Research Design: Qualitative, Quantitative, and Mixed Method Approaches*.

⁹ John W. Creswell, *Research Design: Qualitative, Quantitative, and Mixed Method Approaches*.

¹⁰Exodus 18:19-20. *Access dated March 2015:Ask.com*

capture the attention of the Pastor to present the problem and offer a possible solution for the Associate Minister's behavior. The second challenge was how much time would be needed to conduct a study. The ongoing study included, weekly meetings, one on one setting, individual interviews, and case studies to find the self-interest and passion of each Associate Minister. The issue of which ministry could be chosen and the plan for how the ministry would be led had to be discussed among the Pastor, Associate Minister interested and the President of the Minister's Council. For example, the Homeless Ministry has become the number one ministry.

The Homeless Ministry has generated more noteworthy donations to the homeless population in Maryland and Washington, D.C. The feeding, clothing and shelter for the homeless is the primary duty as missionaries. The interest for church ministries begins with the Pastor, flows to Officers, Members, and outside of the church to the community.

The emphasis that has been placed on the Homeless Ministry is becoming a grounded theory project that will be used outside of the church. It will be presented to other Pastors as a guideline and steps will be used to set up other ministries. B. Glaser states, "Grounded theory is a systematic methodology in the social sciences involving the construction of theory through the analysis of data."[11] Glaser continues, "As researchers review the data collected, repeated ideas, concepts or elements become apparent, and are tagged with codes, which have been extracted from the data. As more data are collected, and as data are re-reviewed, codes can be grouped into concept. Then the data is placed into categories. These categories may become the basis for new theory."[12] The Homeless Ministry has received high visibility in the community. A system providing Community Service has been set up through the Church and services are received from the

---

[11]B. Glaser, Strauss. *The Discovery of Grounded Theory: Strategies for Qualitative Research* (Chicago, IL: Aldine Publication, 1967).

[12]B. Glaser, Strauss. *The Discovery of Grounded Theory: Strategies for Qualitative Research.*

Correction Center of Prince George's County in Capitol Heights, Maryland. The success of the Homeless Ministry can be used as a historical account for the beginning of finding the self-interest and passion for the Associate Ministers. The Miracle Center of Faith Missionary Baptist Church is concerned with missionary duties for members, therefore the Homeless Ministry is a primary concern. It is surprising how observations can reveal so much information. Even the Pastor of The Miracle Center of Faith Missionary Baptist Church has observed that some of the Associate Ministers have a low level of motivation. He has noticed the absence of associate ministers or congregants and will ask the President of the Minister Council, the Researcher, to give a status of each Minister. Upon this request, each Associate Minister must be accounted for. It will be noted that each person is missing for a particular reason. There are times when, the "I don't know" is unacceptable. Each Associate Minister is supposed to alert the Pastor, Diaconate Chairman, and President of the Minister Council of their status, such as, being late, out of town, sickness, death, etc. Any occurrence that causes absentees should be reported and the Pastor should know before all services.

    The Interview collection of data has given in depth information of why Associate Ministers become depressed, uninvolved, uninterested, distracted from the assigned duties that have been given to them. First, when they received their call to ministry, many began to think of preaching to the Congregation. Second, many believed they would become Pastoral Counselors right away. The Qualitative research study was set up with at least five processes to be followed: 1. The Researcher gathered a group of participants together who shared the same characteristics, i.e., Associate Ministers, for the study. 2. A questionnaire was designed that explored the reasoning behind the situation of low motivation levels of the Associate Ministers. The questionnaires were passed to each participant to fill out. The Associate Ministers filled them out and later, approximately two months later, feedback was required to let participants express how each person felt about the new assignments. The feedback was delayed, due to the time used to fill out the questionnaires. There were questions and reactions that had to be addressed before completion of the survey. 3. On the 3rd Sunday, following the second service, a Minister's Council meeting is scheduled. During this meeting, each person is given time to report on their assigned ministry, giving dates, detail of progress, issues encountered, and suggestions for future processes or improvements. 4. The context Pastor spends time every other month in a Sharing session or Focus group that has an agenda to present data and have open discussions. During these sharing sessions certain problems or concerns are solved or designed for further research and responses. 5. Finally, the recorded data from the Sharing session or Focus group is discussed at a higher level in the Diaconate Board Meeting. This meeting is attended by 12 leaders, selected by the Pastor as members to discuss and make policies for the church. There are five Associate Ministers and seven Deacons that handle the overall running of the church and mission fulfillment.

The model for ministry at The Miracle Center of Faith Missionary Baptist began with status reports that record during the month the activities that each Associate Minister has performed, issues encountered, progress made, and future plans. For example, each person does report on the ministry name, their own vision statement, write in a summary statement of goals, and rate themselves on the activities that he or she accomplished during the month. In giving leadership to the chosen ministry, the Associate Minister is striving to become known for the ministry and called upon by the congregation. Further, if community requests or requirements are generated, that named person is the first to be notified by the Pastor. A sample copy of the monthly report will be displayed in the conclusion or appendix of this project. In addition to the monthly report forms, the Associate Ministers are responsible for their personal spiritual growth. Each person must be of "good report" based on Romans 10: 15, "And how shall they preach, except they be sent? As it is written, "How beautiful are the feet of them that preach the gospel of peace and bring glad tidings of good things." Thirdly, the Associate Ministers are encouraged to be a support system for The Miracle Center family members who are grieving and burdened through prayers, phone calls, cards, etc. Galatians 6:2, "Bear ye one another's burdens and so fulfill the law of Christ.

Data Results

Observations

The beginning meetings with the context Pastor of The Miracle Center of Faith Missionary Baptist Church in Capitol Heights, Maryland provided a guideline for future observations. The Pastor has been pleased with the results of the Associate Ministers choosing the ministries that suited their self -interest and passion to lead for the church. There have been some challenges that took time to work out details on how to handle each situation. For example, one Associate Minister leading the Prison Ministry became ill and had to pass her duties to another leader. This was resolved quickly and the program continued the following month. In order to continue the model for ministry the profiles from participants in the church program at the prison were passed on and even more persons began to participate. Perhaps, the male face as a lead was more comfortable for the young males that are in the system. When information is shared, it has become an open forum that appears to be helpful for those in the system and even more helpful to the young males in the church congregation. I have been involved in a ministry called, "Help Before Jail" and this has become more involved and spreading into the community as a way to help young males. A sample profile sheet can be generated or produced through results that can be obtained from Appendix A data. So far, there is positive feedback and ways suggested to give the church and community ideals on how to avoid crimes and help young males make a few extra dollars during after school and during the summer months. Even the introduction to Bible Study has been received well and attitudes toward love for another, respect of God, honor of Father and Mother, and the obeying of authorities has been received and been carried out with success. Each ministry is responsible for having a basic format. The chosen ministries have become somewhat competitive, but the Homeless, Prison, and Youth ministries stand out and receive the most attention. For example, the Youth ministry has involvement during the week, Saturday, and Sunday. There are Youth Advisory Meetings, regular Youth meetings, every other Friday Youth meetings, at least one Saturday outing during the month, and every Sunday. The Sunday youth events include Sunday School, Youth church and some Sundays a food fellowship. The Associate Minister who leads the youth is a busy leader. However, this leader can call or delegate others to assist in needed areas. There are Bible Study leaders, Mentors, Tutors, Culinary, Maintenance, Helping hands, and Entertaining leaders available to lead and teach the youth. The primary focus is on youth, ages four to twelve years old. Further, the infant to three years old are cared for and it has become apparent that those youths twelve to adult, twenty one can become leaders to help the younger children. Then even further, persons over twenty one have become involved, so no one is overlooked. The Youth ministry overflowed over to the Senior ministry, because the seniors did not want to be considered as old. The seniors began to call themselves seasoned and have now become the gentle group that gives wisdom to the youth.

The decision by the Pastor to have the Associate Ministers as lead persons for the self-interest, passion choice ministries has proven, so far to be a great decision. This ideal or plan will continue to go forward and will be presented to other pastors as a model for a motivational tool.

Participants Questionnaires

The model made observations the showed success in helping the Associate Ministers make choices based on their self-interest and passion about particular ministries. Each Associate Minister was assigned a church ministry and continues to give monthly status reports based on the questions asked from the Quarterly Report. The

Quarterly Report was generated monthly during the project study period, June 21. 2013 to October 30, 2013. The fifteen participating Associate Ministers have completed the assigned time. However, since the assigned, there have been occurrences that have taken at least three more ministries to other assignments. One of the ministers has been assigned to another local church in the Maryland area. Also, two others ministers have joined another church, headed by a former Associate Minister of The Miracle Center of Faith Missionary Baptist Church, the context church. The active total of fifteen Associate Ministers ranged in age from twenty six to seventy three years of age. The median age is approximately fifty three based on birthdays that were provided. This data was collected through the one on one sessions/interview and documented for future use. The participants were open to responsibility for regular Church traditions, i.e., Sunday mornings, 7:30 a.m. and 10:00 a.m. services. However, special days, holidays, and 3:00 p.m. services, along with Bible Study and Evening services became the times that Associate Ministers tend to find excuses for rendering services. They begin to tell of family obligations, night driving, job requirements, even a certain amount of rest required to function. If one will read The Associate Minister questionnaire closely, it does state, "Perhaps, Associate Ministers should be given an application for service before taking on the position of Associate Minister." There are ten active females and five active males. However, at any given time, the females will be more present than the males. The context pastor will remark, "it was that way at the tomb of Jesus, early in the morning." All the associates are African American, but sometimes, comments are made about the African culture being present. Also, the Caucasian acting comments may surface in some conversations. It should be noted that since the study, the context church does have a Caucasian minister that had joined the Minister's Council as an Associate. Also, in the building as tenants, there are African/Liberian and African/Jamaican ministers that interact with the context congregation on for scheduled events. Based on the research design by John W. Creswell, the researcher has been able to follow the qualitative method to do interviews, observations, documents, which have developed a solution to solve the motivation problem.

For example, Creswell states, "Thirdly, qualitative researchers uses multiple sources of data or 'typically gather multiple forms of data, such as interviews, observations, and documents, rather than rely on a single data source' which are then reviewed before the researcher makes 'sense of it' and organizes it 'into categories or that cut across all of the data sources.'"[13] From further research, Creswell has provided the extra characteristic of qualitative research as a "holistic account" or a complex picture of the problem or issue under study" and this "involves reporting multiple perspectives, identifying the many factors involved in a situation, and generally sketching the larger picture that emerges."[14] Perhaps, it can be said that problems and issues that have been encountered with the Associate Ministers at The Miracle Center of Faith missionary Baptist Church can be problems and issues in any or other churches. Based on this assumption, it is possible that the steps used to solve the problem and raise the level of motivation for the Associate Ministers can be set forward as a model. The Pastor is used based on the titled project, Solidifying the Relationship Between the Pastor and Associate Ministers. He is used as a defining representative for the Church as Moses was as the leader of the Israelites. Aaron and Miriam are presented as the complaining brother and sister about Moses. The Associate Ministers at The Miracle Center of Faith Missionary Baptist Church, like Aaron and Miriam required defined roles for their duties. The Pastor is known to the congregation and surrounding community for his theoretical knowledge. He is known to quote from theoretical scholars, such as Socrates, Aristotle, Karl Marx, Thomas Aquinas and others. His intellectual roots of critical thinking will sometimes be spoken in a sermon. He develops thoughts, hears from God through visions, and is

---

[13] John W. Creswell, *Research Design: Qualitative, Quantitative, and Mixed Method Approaches* (Thousand Oaks, CA: SAGE Publications, 2009), 175.

[14] John W. Creswell, *Research Design: Qualitative, Quantitative, and Mixed Method Approaches,* 176.

then found to grow with an action plan to set out plans according to what "Thus saith the Lord."[15] He is a firm believer in hearing from the Lord and establishing a plan on solid ground. The solid ground of scripture is his basis for leading the congregation. The Pastor, like Moses, waits to hear from God when making a decision.

The primary scripture for Old Testament foundation is Numbers 12. Numbers 12:6 states, "And he said, Hear now my words: If there be a prophet among you, I the Lord will make myself known unto him in a vision, and will speak unto him in a dream." The Researcher cannot think of any failure in the Pastor. However, the Congregation has failed to live up to some of his expectations. In this situation, it can be considered as a failure, he has a heart to forgive. Like Jesus, he may say, "Father, forgive them, for they know not what they do."[16] When those situations occur, he is careful to have a work around plan and continues to move forward. For example, when the Associate Ministers do not step up for assignments or unavailable, the Pastor will assign the duties to Deacons. The Pastor is known to be an encourager. He will help any person find or see potential in him or herself. He has studied psychology and has the ability to motivate people. Many testimonies are told during events, i.e., upcoming 23rd Anniversary, the past Family and Friends Day, and upcoming 40th Anniversary, June 9, 2014 will be times of testimonies. These are times when one can find out about the Theological foundations that have been set at The Miracle Center of Faith Missionary Baptist Church. The Pastor is equipped to teach as well as preach.

With regard to theory and practice, Christ is in the midst of all foundation requirements, i.e. Biblical, Historical, Theological, and Theoretical. Each foundation has shown concepts, methods, and confirm the Gospel, Good News of Jesus Christ. Thought the context of The Miracle Center of Faith Missionary Baptist Church the gospel is based on the Baptist religion to build the foundation of the Apostles and Prophets. Matthew 16:13-20 let's one know that Jesus asked his

---

[15] Lord.pdf, access date March 2015, www.letgodbetrue.com/pdf/thus-saith-the-lord.pdf Study, "Thus saith the Lord," occur 413 times in the Bible.

[16] Biblehub.com/luke/23-34.htm.

Disciples, "Whom do men say that I am?" Then Peter, answering said, "Thou are the loving Christ, son of the living God..." The Miracle Center of Faith Missionary Baptist Church embraces this Theological foundation as the basis for serving God and integrating all of the Christian theology. Even further, is the embracing of the Holy Ghost on the day of Pentecost, Acts 1: 11... While studying the Epistles of Paul, one does ask the question, "What can I do to please God?" What am I allowed to do for pleasure in this world? Paul would note in Philippians 2:3, one more important than yourself, ... not selfishness. Colossians 3:5...deal with greed...idolatry... whereas, Romans 12:10 deals with one another... own profit,...vs profit of many (1 Corinthians 6:20). Then, to continue, pray at all times, Luke 18:1, serve the Living God (Hebrews 9;13), and edify your neighbor (Romans 15:2)... As man and woman try to reach heaven from this earthly state will always be concerned about the Kingdom of God and what can one do to reach the Kingdom as the final and everlasting destination. Further, as the project is researched on "What can motivate the Associate Minister to support the Pastor and help the Congregation, while maintaining a high level of motivation for oneself." Possibly, the self-interest and passion for the assignment will be the basis for creating the steps to keep the Associate Ministers motivated. Since, every knee will bow and every tongue will confess Jesus Christ, it is a good thing for Associate Ministers to be motivated to the highest level possible. At this time, a Survey has been prepared, in work, reviewed, and continuing to receive views and questions that lead to farther research. The Associate Ministers were shocked that such a Study and research is being done that involves the observation of them and require responds from them. It appears that when persons know they are part of a study, attitudes improve, questions and concerns arise. This is a positive reaction, however, it can also, be a negative reaction. Second, it will be shown that Case Studies will provide meaning answers for questions about motivation and answers to how to deal with motivation for the Associate Ministers. More will take place to steps that can be used by The Miracle Center of Faith Missionary Baptist

Church and any other Church or Organization that require support from followers. Followers should realize that they are also, Leaders, but in a role that has a higher Leader. As man and woman try to reach heaven from this earthly state will always be concerned about the Kingdom of God and what can one do to reach the Kingdom as the final and everlasting destination.

Risk Factors
- 10 percent of the associate ministers are inactive, due to sickness, jobs, or family obligations.
- 10 percent of associate ministers will find excuses and resist doing the questionnaire, survey or participate in the one-on-interview.
- 10 percent will not be totally honest in responding to inquires or questions.

Hypothesis

The defined hypothesis is the associate ministers do not have a clear understanding of their call to ministry. The call to ministry does not just mean a chance to preach, it entails the need to serve. Douglas Brown's, *"The Call to the Ministry"* stated, "The disturbing reality is that fewer people are committing themselves to vocational Christian ministry. Why is this the case? I believe part of the problem rests in the fundamental misunderstanding concerning the call of God."[17] "Simply put, the call to ministry is God's sovereign selection of individuals for full-time, vocational service."[18] "Ideally, the call is a lifetime appointment in which one devotes himself to the ministry and makes it his livelihood."[19] "Throughout redemptive history, God has called individuals into His service to fulfill His purposes."[20] Therefore, associate ministers should be prepared to serve. The pastor is the

---

[17]Doulas Brown, Ph.D., access date January 2016, www.ask.com, *The Call to the Ministry* (Ankeny, IO: Faith Pulpit), 2008.
[18]Douglas Brown, Ph.D, *The Call to the Ministry*.
[19]Douglas Brown, Ph.D, *The Call to the Ministry*.
[20]Douglas Brown, Ph.D, *The Call to the Ministry*.

visionary leader and gives direction for the support from associate ministers.

Project Calendar

From the time of proposing a project, there was a need to raise the level of motivation for the Associate Ministers in the context Church. Upon speaking with the context Pastor of The Miracle Center of Faith Missionary Baptist Church, the need was concurred. Following the meeting, a plan was laid out to have scheduled meetings and to conduct a survey. The Survey consisted of eight questions about the Associate Minister's self-interest and passion for ministry. Also, the Associate Ministers had to write an essay about their experience with other Churches, your call to Ministry, and your expectations from this venture as Associate Minister. This Questionnaire/Survey was given to the Associate Ministers during a monthly meeting, the 3rd Sunday in June 2014, following the 10:00 a.m. Sunday Worship Service.

The weekly meetings were scheduled for at least eight weeks, since June 21, 2013, to October 30,.2013. The Associate Ministers were given the summer months to reflect and get ready for the fall sessions. The training consisted of discussing faithfulness, commitment, and consistency, as requirements for becoming the leader of a particular ministry. In these weekly meetings, the Associate Ministers were given handouts of various Scripture, such as, Jesus washing the feet of the disciples, John 13:5. During these weekly meetings, each person would give a two minute meaning of what service to the Pastor and Congregation meant to him or her. The Pastor of The Miracle Center of Faith Missionary Baptist Church is known for being Business Minded in Jesus. His teaching can be found in the writings of John C. Maxwell. John C. Maxwell, wrote, "People are never successful by talent alone. Rather, great leaders develop through a process of discipline, hard work, diligence, and steady self-improvement." These weekly Meetings have created a purpose for Associate Ministers to be active and have purpose for their positions.

Since these meetings, the Associate Ministers have become more supportive to the Pastor and more attentive to the Congregation.

In the context location in Capitol Heights, Maryland, The Miracle Center of Faith Missionary Baptist consist of eighteen Associate Ministers. One Associate Minister is in the Nursing Home. However, during a visit, in support of the Project, certain questions were asked and his responses are recorded as an Interview instead of a Survey. Also, there are two retired Pastors that are now Associate Ministers, who were interviewed. Further, a six month, Internship Student, Associate Minister was interviewed. During the six to eight week Study, two Associate Ministers have relocated to a Church, in another area of Capitol Heights, Maryland. One of the Associate Ministers is reported as a Case Study in the Theological Foundation.

In order to raise the level of motivation the Associate Ministers have been given the lead of President of the Church Ministry, i.e., Homeless Ministry, Nursing Home Ministry, Prison Ministry, Job Placement Ministry, Evangelism Ministry, Outreach Ministry, Sick Visitation Ministry, Audio and Video Ministry, Youth Ministry, Senior Ministry, Social Action Ministry, etc. Training is being provided to the Associate Ministers, such as, Baptism, Communion, Baby Dedication, Funeral Procession, Praying, Reading Scripture, Call to Worship, Opening the Doors of the Church, etc. The process of defining the roles of the Associate Ministers brings them to know that there service is recognized by the pastor and congregation.

In conclusion, it has been shown that when persons become active and more involved, they are motivated to do more. From the John Maxwell, 21 Irrupted Laws of leadership, as a guideline, along with the Bible Scriptures, it has been shown that the Associate Ministers can become faithful, committed, and consistent in serving to support the Pastor and serve the Congregation and Community, as leaders of the aforementioned Church Ministries. As Leaders of the various Ministries, each Associate Minister becomes active, responsible, and must provide a monthly status during the Minister's Council Meeting, every 3rd Sunday, following the 10:00 a.m. Morning Worship Service. The status reports that record during the month the activities that each

Associate Minister has performed, issues encountered, progress made, and future plans is a challenge. For example, each person does report on the ministry name, their own vision statement, write in a summary statement of goals, and rate themselves on the activities that he or she accomplished during the month. In giving leadership to the chosen ministry, the Associate Minister is striving to become known for the ministry and called upon by the congregation. It is a challenge for me to keep a record when Associate Ministers do not present their reports in a timely manner. Further, if community requests or requirements are generated, that named person is the first to be notified by the Pastor. A sample copy of the monthly report can be generated upon request for this project. In addition to the monthly report forms, the Associate Ministers are responsible for their personal spiritual growth.

As a leader and President of the Minister's Council, I have spent three years at the United Theological Seminary in Dayton, Ohio and other assigned locations obtaining spiritual information and interacting with persons who share similar experiences. As time pass, these methods or steps will be documented for future use by other Pastors for their Associate Ministers." I have learned through this experience that there will more than likely always be an issue in churches. Perhaps, the similar issue dealing with Associate Ministers who only want to preach, rather than serve or another issue. Whether, this or another, the process or model of ministry can be replicated or used to generate a similar solidifying or defining of roles to generate a understanding between the Pastor and Associate Ministers. In conversations that have occurred between other Ministers, for example the Minister's Council of the American Baptist Churches of the South it has been brought to their attention. The Pastors have stated similar issues with their Associate Ministers. Therefore, this project or final document will be discussed and further developed.

APPENDIX A

QUESTIONNAIRE / SURVEY

QUESTIONNAIRE / SURVEY

The Questionnaire, Survey was titled, The Associate Minister. The information was presented as follows:
>What are your interests?
>What are your schedules?
>Are you called to the ministry by God?

The position is manmade, but the calling to ministry should be from God. It should be an honor to be an Associate Minister. One should consider him or herself in a holding position. The holding position may possibly lead to a Pastoral position. In the meantime, the Associate Minister should perform to the highest level possible. The Associate Minister should be gifted or at least trainable, and have a reflectable/good attitude for service. The Associate Minister can be responsible for the following:

- The Church traditions… First Sunday
- Dr. Martin Luther King's Birthday
- Valentine's Day
- President's Day
- Palm Sunday
- Easter
- Brainstorming Worship topics
- Church values and congregational responsibilities
- Vocation (Summer Camp/Vacation Bible School)
- Personal Integration (Follow your Dreams)
- The Common Good (love One Another)
- Must have moral authority.

Perhaps, Associate Ministers should be given an applicant for service before taking on the position of Associate Minister. When a person is given a position that satisfies their self-interest, they usually will be confident.

1. Do you understand the position of Associate Minister?

2. Are you willing to serve as Associate Minister as a faithful, committed, and consistent person?
3. Are you familiar with the administration of this Church, i.e., The Miracle Center of Faith Missionary Baptist Church?
4. Are you willing to walk, shadow, and follow directions from the Pastor?

Follow the Pastor's Lead…

Please write a short essay about your experience with other churches, your call to ministry, and your expectations from this venture as Associate Minister.

In conclusion, this is a designed approach that ongoing for the implementation of a project within The Miracle Center of Faith Missionary Baptist Church.

APPENDIX B

PRE AND POST TEST QUESTIONNAIRE

PRE AND POST TEST QUESTIONNAIRE

Pre-Test/Post Test: Respondents will be asked to rate on a scale of 1-5, **1 – Always   2 – Most of the Time   3 – Sometimes   4 – Seldom   5 – Never**

_____ 1. Do you feel comfortable as an associate minister?
_____ 2. Are you satisfied with the schedule for Sunday services?
_____ 3. Are you comfortable working as a team to do ministry?
_____ 4. I believe I am in the right position for church ministry.
_____ 5. I prefer to work with only one other person.
_____ 6. I feel as if I am not understood.
_____ 7. I am uncomfortable dealing with the congregation.
_____ 8. I believe I can do more for the church.
_____ 9. My concerns and suggestion are not addressed by the pastor.
_____ 10. I prefer to only receive assignments from the pastor.

APPENDIX C
ASSOCIATE MINISTER'S TRAINING CLASS

ASSOCIATE MINISTER'S TRAINING CLASS

Training Class should include the following:
- Preaching Styles
- Reading of Scritpure – King James Version and other translations
- Weddings
- Funerals
- The Lord's Suppoer or Communion for believers
- Baptism
- Baby Deidications

APPENDIX D

SAMPLE CODE OF ETHICS

Sample "Code of Ethics"

This sample is taken from the text *Ministerial Ethics:* Moral Formation for Church Leaders co-authored by Joe E. Trull and James E. Carter (Grand Rapids: Baker Academic, 2004), 259-263. Where also is found many other ministerial codes in the Appendices (217-263).

Appendix IV
Sample Codes of Ethics ((1))
Pastor or Senior Minister Code

(Includes basic obligations for all ministers)

Preamble

As a minister of Jesus Christ, called by God to proclaim the gospel and gifted by the Spirit to pastor the church, I dedicate myself to conduct my ministry according to the ethical guidelines and principles set forth in this code of ethics, in order that my ministry be acceptable to God, my service be beneficial to the Christian community, and my life be a witness to the world.

Responsibilities to Self

1. I will maintain my physical and emotional health through regular exercise, good eating habits, and the proper care of my body.

2. I will nurture my devotional life through a regular time of prayer, reading of the Scriptures, and meditation.

3. I will continue to grow intellectually through personal study, comprehensive reading, and attending growth conferences.

4. I will manage my time well by properly balancing personal obligations, church duties, and family responsibilities, and by observing a weekly day off and an annual vacation.

5. I will be honest and responsible in my finances by paying all debts on time, never seeking special gratuities or privileges, giving generously to worthwhile causes, and living a Christian lifestyle.

6. I will be truthful in my speech, never plagiarizing another's work, exaggerating the facts, misusing personal experiences, or communicating gossip.

7. I will seek to be Christ-like in attitude and action toward all persons regardless of race, social class, religious beliefs, or position of influence within the church and community.

Responsibilities to Family

1. I will be fair to every member of my family, giving them the time, love, and consideration they need.

2. I will understand the unique role of my spouse, recognizing his or her primary responsibility is as marital partner and parent to the children, and secondarily as church worker and assistant to the pastor.

3. I will regard my children as a gift from God and seek to meet their individual needs without imposing undue expectations upon them.

Responsibilities to the Congregation

1. I will seek to be a servant-minister of the church by following the example of Christ in faith, love, wisdom, courage, and integrity.

2. I will faithfully discharge my time and energies as pastor, teacher, preacher, and administrator through proper work habits and reasonable schedules.

3. In my administrative and pastoral duties, I will be impartial and fair to all members.

4. In my preaching responsibilities, I will give adequate time to prayer and preparation, so that my presentation will be biblically based, theologically correct, and clearly communicated.

5. In my pastoral counseling, I will maintain strict confidentiality, except in cases where disclosure is necessary to prevent harm to persons and/or is required by law.

6. In my evangelistic responsibilities, I will seek to lead persons to salvation and to church membership without manipulating converts, proselytizing members of other churches, or demeaning other religious faiths.

7. In my visitation and counseling practices, I will never be alone with a person of another sex unless another church member is present nearby.

8. I will not charge fees to church members for weddings or funerals; for nonmembers I will establish policies based on ministry opportunities, time constraints, and theological beliefs.

9. As a full-time minister, I will not accept any other remunerative work without the expressed consent of the church.

10. In leaving a congregation, I will seek to strengthen the church through proper timing, verbal affirmation, and an appropriate closure of my ministry.

Responsibilities to Colleagues

1. I will endeavor to relate to all ministers, especially those with whom I serve in my church, as partners in the work of God, respecting their ministry and cooperating with them.

2. I will seek to serve my minister colleagues and their families with counsel, support, and personal assistance.

3. I will refuse to treat other ministers as competition in order to gain a church, receive an honor, or achieve statistical success.

4. I will refrain from speaking disparagingly about the person or work of any other minister, especially my predecessor or successor.

5. I will enhance the ministry of my successor by refusing to interfere in any way with the church I formerly served.

6. I will return to a former church field for professional services, such as weddings and funerals, only if invited by the resident pastor.

7. I will treat with respect and courtesy any predecessor who returns to my church field.

8. I will be thoughtful and respectful to all retired ministers and, upon my retirement, I will support and love my pastor.

9. I will be honest and kind in my recommendations of other ministers to church positions or other inquiries.

10. If aware of serious misconduct by a minister, I will contact responsible officials of that minister's church body and inform them of the incident.

Responsibility to the Community

1. I will consider my primary responsibility is to be pastor of my congregation and will never neglect ministerial duties in order to serve in the community.

2. I will accept reasonable responsibilities for community service, recognizing the minister has a public ministry.

3. I will support public morality in the community through responsible prophetic witness and social action.

4. I will obey the laws of my government unless they require my disobedience to the law of God.

5. I will practice Christian citizenship without engaging in partisan politics or political activities that are unethical, unbiblical, or unwise.

Responsibilities to my Denomination

1. I will love, support and cooperate with the faith community of which I am a part, recognizing the debt I owe to my denomination for its contribution to my life, my ministry, and my church.

2. I will work to improve my denomination in its efforts to expand and extend the kingdom of God.

Associate Minister Code ((2))
(Education/Music/Youth/Etc.)

- I will be supportive and loyal to the senior pastor or, if unable to do so, will seek another place of service.
- I will be supportive and loyal to my fellow staff ministers, never criticizing them or undermining their ministry.
- I will recognize my role and responsibility on the church staff and will not feel threatened or in competition with other ministers of my special area of ministry.
- If single, I will be discreet in my dating practices, especially in relation to members of my congregation.

Pastoral Counselor Code ((3))

- I will have a pastor/counselor to whom I can turn for counseling and advice.

- I will be aware of my own needs and vulnerabilities, never seeking to meet my own needs through my counselees.
- I will recognize the power I hold over counselees and never take advantage of their vulnerability through exploitation or manipulation.
- I will never become sexually or romantically involved with a client, or engage in any form of erotic or romantic conduct.
- I will demonstrate unconditional acceptance and love toward all counselees, regardless of their standards, beliefs, attitudes, or actions.
- If I am unable to benefit a client, I will refer him or her to another professional
  - who can provide appropriate therapy.
- I will maintain good relationships with other counselors and therapists, informing and conferring with them about mutual concerns.
- I will keep confidential all matters discussed in a counseling setting, unless the information is hazardous for the client, for another person, or is required by law.
- I will offer my assistance and services to fellow ministers and their families whenever needed.
- I will support and contribute to the ministry of my church through personal counseling, seminars, lectures, workshops, and group therapy.
- I will seek to support the policies and beliefs of my church without unduly imposing them upon any counselee.

Military Chaplain Code ((4))

I will be an ethical example of a Christian lifestyle in a military setting.

- I will perform my service duties according to the military codes of conduct, Recognizing my ultimate allegiance is to God.

- I will be truthful in my reports to my senior officers without divulging unnecessary confidential information.

Notes

((1)) These sample codes are generic examples of numerous ministerial codes and they have been edited to include the most significant emphases, both principles and specific guidelines, in each category. To write a code, a minister should evaluate his or her own ministry obligations in light of the text discussions, then utilize these sample codes as broad statements of possibilities for a personal code of ministerial ethics.

((2)) The "Sample Codes" of the associate ministers and others which follow will include only those obligations in additions to the Senior Minister Code, which uniquely apply to each special ministerial role.

((3)) See appendix III for the Code of the Christian Association of Psychologists and Counselors, which, although it has many obvious weakness, does deal with the primary issues facing pastoral counselors.

((4)) These statements have been suggested by military chaplains as additions to the basic code for ministers.

[Many thanks to Cheryl Reagan for typing the code from a FAXed copy.]
Updated

BIBLIOGRAPHY

Applegate, Debby. *The Most Famous Man in America.* New York, NY: Doubleday Religious Publishing Group, 2007.

Armitage, Thomas. *History of the Baptist; Traced by Their Vital Principles and Practices.* Broadway, NY: Bryan, Taylor, & Co., 1887.

Baker, Robert A. *A Summary of Christian History.* Nashville, TN: Broodman Press, Reproduced by permission. Copyright., 1959.

Berhof, Louis. *Introduction to Systematic Theology.* Eerdmans publishing, 1932. Reprint edition: Grand Rapids: Baker, MI, 1979.

Billingsley, Barbara, Lowe, Diana and Stratton, Mary (2006).*Civil Justice System and the Public Learning from Experiences to find Practices that Work.* May 2006. CJSP Report. Available online: http://cfcj-fcjc.org/docs/2006/cjsp-learning-en.pdf

Blanchard, Ken. *The Servant Leader* Nashville, TN: Thomas Nelson, 2003.

Bloesch, Donald G. *Essentials of Evangelical theology.* 2 Vols., Harper & Row, New York, NY, 1978-79

Boehner, Philotheus. *Bonaventure, The Journey of the Mind to God.* Hackett Publishing Co., Indianapolis, IN, 1993.

Boice, James Montgomery. *Foundations of the Christian Faith.* Revised one-volume edition. Intervarsity Press, Downers Grove, IL, 1986.

Butler, Joseph. *The Analogy of Religion, Natural and Revealed, to the Constitution and Course of Nature.* Scholarly Publishing Office, University of Michigan Library, Ann Arbor, MI, 2005.

Buswell, James Oliver, Jr. *A Systematic Theology of the Christian Religion,* 2 vols. Zondervan, Grand Rapids, MI, 1962-63.

Calvin, John. Institutes of the Christian Religion. 2 vols. Ed. by John T. McNeil. Trans.and Indexed by Fred Lewis Battles. *The Library of Christian Classics,* Westminster, PA, 1960.

Campbell, Donald & Stanley, Julian *Experimental and Quasi-Experimental Designs for Research.* Boston, MA: Houghton Mifflin Company, 1963.

Carpenter, Joel A. *Revive Us Again: The Reawakening of American Fundamentalism.* Oxford University Press. New York, NY, 1997.

Chrislip, David D., & Larson, Carl E. *Collaborative Leadership: How Citizens and Civic Leaders can Make a Difference* San Francisco, CA: Jossey-Bass, 1994.

Clark, Samuel. *A Demonstration of the Being and Attributes of God: And Other Writings.* Ed. Vailato, Ezio. Cambridge University Press, 1998.

Clinton, J. Robert. *Leadership Development theory: Comparative Studies Among High level Christian Leaders* (Unpublished doctoral dissertation). Fuller Theological Seminary, Pasadena, California, 1988.

——— *The Making of a Leader.* Colorado Springs, CO: Navpress, 1988.

——— *Leadership Emergence Theory*. Madison, WI: Printing Plus, 1989.

Common English Bible. *www.Common English Bible.com* Nashville, TN: Library of Congress Cataloging-in-Publication Data, 2011.

Cowan M. *Introduction to Practical Theology*. Online article: Institute for Ministry, Loyola University. www.loyno.edu/~mcowan/PracticalTheology.html, 2008.

Craig, William Lane. *The Cosmological Argument from Plato to Leibniz*. Barnes & Noble Books, New York, NY, 1980.

Creswell, John W. *Research Design, Qualitative & Quantitative Approaches*. Thousand Oaks, CA. Sage Publications, Inc., 1994.

Congar, Yves. *A History of Theology*. Doubleday. New York, NY, 1968.

Copeland, K. Edward. *Riding in the Second Chariot*. Rockford, IL: Prayer Closet Publishing, 2004.

Cranton, Patricia. *Professional Development as Transformative Learning: New Perspective for Teachers of Adults*. San Francisco: Jossey-Bass1996.

Curry LA, Nembhard IM, Bradley EH. *Qualitative and Mixed Methods Provide Unique Contributions to Outcomes Research*, 2009.

Dabney, Robert L. *Discussions: Evangelical and Theological*. Reprint of 1980 Ed. Banner of Truth, London, 1967.

Dahlberg K, Dahlberg H, Nyström M. *Reflective Lifeworld Research*, 2nd Ed. Lund, Studentlitteratur, 2008.

Damazio, Frank. *The Making of a Leader* Portland, OR: City Bible Publishing, 1988.

Denzin, Norman K., & Yvonna S. Lincoln. *Entering the Field of Qualitative Research.* Thousand Oaks, CA: Sage Publications, Inc.,1994.

———. *Handbook of qualitative research* (pp. 1-17). Thousand Oaks, CA: Sage Publications Inc., 1994.

———. *Strategies of qualitative inquiry* (2nd ed.). Thousand Oaks, CA: Sage Publications Inc., 2003.

Dick, Bob. *A Beginner's Guide to Action Research* [On line]. Available at http://www.scu.edu.au/schools/gcm/ar/arp/guide.html., 2000.

Dillman, Don A. Smythe, Jolene D. & Christian, Leah Melani. *Internet, Mail and Mixed-Mode Surveys: the Tailored Design Method.* New York, NY: Wiley, 2008.

Dooyeweerd, H. *In the Twilight of Western Thought.* Philadelphia, PA: The Presbyterian Reformed Publishing Company, 1960.

Driscoll M. *The Church and the Supremacy of Christ in a Postmodern World.* In J. Piper and T. Justin (Ed), *The Supremacy of Christ in a Postmodern* World Wheaton, IL: Crossway Books, 2007.

Eavey C. Principles of Teaching for Christian Teachers, Grand Rapids, MI: Zondervan, 1940.

Edlin, Richard J. & J. Ireland (Eds.), *Engaging the Culture: Christians at Work in Education* Blacktown, NSW: National Institute for Christian Education.

Edwards, Jonathan. *The Works of Jonathan Edwards.* 2 vols. Revised and corrected by Edward Hickman. Edinburgh: Banner of Truth, 1974.

Eisner, Elliot W. *The Enlightened Eye: Qualitative Inquiry and the Enhancement of Educational Practice.* Upper Saddle River, NJ: Merrill, 1998.

Erickson, Millard. *Christian Theology.* Grand Rapids, MI: Baker Books, 1985.

Evans, James H. *We Have Been Believers: An African American Systematic Theology.* Minneapolis, MN: Fortress Press, 1992.

Fields, Theodore P. *All the Pastor's Men: The Associate Minister in the Black Church Setting.* Bloomington, IN: Authorhouse, 2002.

Fowler, Floyd J. *Improving Survey Questions: Design and Evaluation. Survey Methodology.* Newbury Park, CA: Sage, 1995.

Fullan, Michael. *Leading in a Culture of Change.* San Francisco, CA: Jossey-Bass, 2001.

Gangel, Kenneth O., & Howard G. Hendrick. *The Christian Educator's Handbook on Teaching.* Grand Rapids, MI: Baker Books, 1988.

George, Carl F. Bird, Warren. *How to Break Growth Barriers.* Grand Rapids, MI: Baker Book House, 1993.

———. *Prepare Your Church for the Future.* Grand Rapids, MI: Fleming H. Revell/Baker Books, 1992.

Glaser, Barney G., & Strauss, Amselm L. *The Discovery of Rounded Theory: Strategies for Qualitative Research.* Chicago, IL: Aldine Transaction, 1967.

Goodwin, C. James. *Research in Psychology: Methods and Design.* USA: John Wiley & Sons, Inc, 2005.

Green, Richard. Boethius, *The Consolation of Philosophy.* Macmillan Publishing Co., New York, NY, 1962.

Greenleaf, Robert. K. *Servant Leadership: A Journey into the Nature of Legitimate Power and Greatness.* Mahwah, NJ: Paulist Press, 1977.

———. *The Servant as Leader.* Indianapolis, IN: The Robert K. Greenleaf Center, 1991.

Grudem, Wayne, Grudem. *Systematic Theology: An Introduction to Biblical Doctrine.* England, UK: Inter-varsity Press, 1994.
Hansen, David. *The Art of Pastoring.* Downers Grove, IL: InterVarsity Press. 2012Holness, Dr. E. Gail. Lessons In Truth: Selected Sermons. Washington, DC: Precise Communications, 2006.

Hawkins, Martin and Salliman. *The Associate Pastor: Second Chair, Not Second Best* Nashville, TN: Broadman and Holman Publishers, 2005.

Hayes Edward L. *Theological Foundations of Adult Christian Education.* In G.A., 1970.

Heitink, Gerben. *Practical Theology: History, Theory, Action Domains: Manual for Practical Theology.* Grand Rapids, MI: Wm. B. Eerdmans Publishing, 1999.

Helseth, P. K. *Christ-Centered, Bible-Based, and Second-Rate? Right Reason as the Aesthetic Foundation of Christian Education.* Westminster Theological Journal, 69(2), 2007.

Henry, Matthew. *Matthew Henry's Concise Commentary on the Whole Bible.* Nashville: Thomas Nelson Inc., 2000.

Hibbs, Thomas. *Dialectic and Narrative in Aquinas: An Interpretation of the Summa Contra Gentiles.* University of Notre Dame Press, 1995.

Hiscox, Edward. *Principles and Practices for Baptist Churches* Grd Rapids, MI: Kregal Publications, 1980.

Hopewell, David K. Sr. *Becoming an Effective Associate Minister and Church Leader* Lithonia, GA: Orman Press Inc., 2004.

Horne H. *Jesus the Teacher* revised A Gunn, Grand Rapids, MI: Kregel Publication, 1998.

Hubbard, Doulas W. *How to Measure Anything, 2nd edition.* New York: John Wiley and Sons, 2010.

Hughes, Richard L; Beatty, Katherine M. *Becoming a Strategic Leader: Your Role in Your Organization's Enduring Success.* San Francisco, CA: Jossey-Bass, 2005.

Hume, David. An Enquiry Concerning Human Understanding. Hackett Publishing Co., Indianapolis, IN, 1977.

Iorg, Jeff. *The Character of Leadership* Nashville, TN: B & H Publishing, 2007.

Jakes, T.D.; Miller, Stanley. *When Shepherds Bleed*. Charleston, WV: Pneuma Life Publishing, 1995.

Jeremias, Joachim. *New Testament Theology The Proclamation of Jesus* translated by John Bowden, New York, NY: SCM-Canterbury Press Ltd., 1971.

Kant, Immanuel. *Critique of Pure Reason*. trans. Smith, Norman Kemp. St. Martin's Press. New York, NY, 1929.

Kenny, Anthony. *The Five Ways: St. Thomas Aquinas' Proofs of the Existence of God.* Routledge & K. Paul., London, 1969.

Langdridge D. *Phenomenological Psychology: Theory, Research and Method*. Harlow, Pearson Prentice Hall, 2007.

Larkin M, Watts S, Clifton E. *Giving Voice and Making Sense in Interpretative Phenomenological Analysis*. Qualitative Research in Psychology, 2006.

Lawrence, Bill; *Effective Pastoring: Giving Vision, Direction, and Care to Your Church.* Nashville, TN: Thomas Nelson, 1999.

Lincoln, Yvonna. S. & Guba, Egon. G. *Naturalistic Inquiry.* Beverly Hills, CA: Sage Publications Inc., 1985.

Locke, John. *An Essay Concerning Human Understanding*. Oxford University Press, 1975.

Lockyer, Herbert. *All the Women of the Bible.* Grand Rapids, MI: Zondervan, 1988.

London, H. B. Jr. *The Heart of a Great Pastor* Ventura, CA: Regal Books, 1994.

MacArthur, John. *Called to Lead.* Nashville, TN: Thomas Nelson, 2004.

MacKenna, Stephen. *Plotinus, Enneads*. New York, NY: Larson Publications, 1992.

Mas, Jimmy. *Developing the Deaconate: A Manual for Training Secondary Leaders.* Sunrise, FL: Character Craft Publications, 1991.

Maxwell, John C. *The 21 Indispensable Qualities of a Leader: Becoming the Person Others will Want to Follow.* Nashville, TN: Thomas Nelson, Inc., 1999.

———. *The Maxwell Leadership Bible* Nashville, TN: Thomas Nelson Inc., 2002.

Mays, Nicholas and Pope. Catherine. *Qualitative Research in Health Care: Assessing Quality in Qualitative Research*, Malden, MA: Blackwell Publishing Ltd., 2000.

McFague Sallie. *Speaking in Parables,* Philadelphia, PA: Fortress Press, 1975.

McKim Donald K. *Westminster Dictionary of Theological Terms.* Louisville, KY: Westminster John Knox Press, 1996.

Melton, J. Gordon. *Religions of the World Second Edition: A Comprehensive Encyclopedia of Beliefs and Practices,* 2010.

Merriam-Webster Online Dictionary. Online article:

http://www.merriam-webster.com/dictionary, 2008.

Metzger, Bruce M. *The Interpreter's Study Bible*. Nashville, TN: Abingdon Press, 2003.

Miles, Matthew B., and Michael Huberman. *Qualitative Data Analysis: An Expanded Sourcebook. 2nd. Edition.* Thousand Oaks, CA: Sage Publications, 1994.

Miller, George A.; Galanter, Eugene & Pribram, Karl H. *Plans and the Structure of Behaviour.* New York: Holt, Rinehart and Winston, 1960.

Mitchell, Henry H. *Black Church Beginnings: The Long-Hidden Realities of the First Years.* Grand Rapids, MI: William B. Eerdmans Publishing Co., 2004.

Musser, Donald W. and Joseph L. Price. *A New Handbook of Christian Theology.* Nashville, TN: Abingdon Press, 1992.

New American Standard Bible. The Lockman Foundation. Electronic edition STEP Files. Cedar Rapids, IA: Parsons Technology, 1995.

New International Version. International Bible Society. Electronic edition STEP Files. Cedar Rapids, IA: Parsons Technology, 1984.

Noll, Mark A. *The Scandal of the Evangelical Mind.* B. Eerdmans Publishing Co., 1994.

Oden, Thomas. *The Living God. System Theology, Vol. 1.* Harper & Row. San Francisco, CA, 1987.

Packard, Stephen. *Theology Foundations for Collaborative Ministry. Explorations in Practical, Pastoral and Empirical Theology.* Oxford Centre for Ecclesiology and Practical Theology. UK, 2009.

Packer, James I. *Concise Theology:A Guide to Historic Christian Beliefs*. Wheaton, IL: Tyndale House Publishers, 1993.

Park, HiRho Y.; Willhauck, Susan. *Breaking Through the Stained Glass Ceiling.* Nashville, TN: The United Methodist Church, 2013.

Patton, Michael Q. *Qualitative Evaluation and Research Methods (2nd Edition).* Thousand Oaks, CA: Sage Publications Inc., 2001.

Petersen, David L., Gaventa, Beverly R. *The New Interpreter's One Bible Volume Commentary on the Bible*. Editorial Board. Abingdon Press, 2010.

Plantinga, Alvin. *God and Other Minds*. Cornell University Press, 1967.

Polkinghorne, John C. *Belief in God in an Age of Science.* New Haven, CT: Yale University Press, 1998.

Proctor, Samuel DeWitt. *The Substance of Things Hoped For: A Memoir of African- American Faith.* New York, Valley Forge, PA: Judson Press, 1995.

Radcliffe, Robert J. *Effective Ministry as an Associate Pastor: Making Beautiful Music as a Ministry Team.* Grand Rapids, MI: Kregel Publications, 1998.

Rath, Tom; Conchie, Barry. *Strength Based Leadership: Great Leaders, Teams, and Why People Follow.* New York, NY: Gallup Press, 2008.

Rideger, Lloyd G. Clery Killers: Guidance for Pastors and Congregations Under Attack New York, NY: Westminister John Knox Press, 1997.

Richards, Larry. *The Bible: God's Word for the Biblically Inept Series.* Lancaster, PA: Starburst Publishers, 1994.

Ritchie, Jane , Ormston, Rachel, *A Guide for Social Science Students and Researchers* Los Angeles, CA: SAGE Publishing, 2013.

Robinson James M. *The Jesus Seminar-Liberal theologians investigating the life of Jesus:* Online article: Ontario Consultants on Religious Tolerance, 2007. www.religioustolerance.org/chr_jsem.htm, 2008.

Stratton, Mary . *Action Research: Teaching and Learning in Motion.* CUEXPO 2008 Paper. http://cfcj-fcjc.org/docs/2008/cjsp-cuexpo-en.pdf.

Strauss, Anselm and Corbin, Juliet. *Basics of Qualitative Research: Grounded Theory Procedures and Techniques.* Newbury Park, CA: Sage Publications Inc., 1990.

Strong's Exhaustive Concordance. Parsons Technology, Electronic edition STEP Files. Cedar Rapids, IA: Parsons Technology.

Schwandt, A. Thomas. *Qualitative Inquiry: A Dictionary of Terms.* London: Sage, 1997.

Schön, David. *The Reflective Practitioner: How Professionals Think in Action.* Basic Books 1983.

Stringfellow, Alan B. Dr. *Great Characters of the Bible* Tulsa, OK: Hensley Publishing 1980.

Stump, Eleonore. *Philosophy of Religion*. Blackwell Publishers. Malden, MA 1999.

Sukienniuk, Diane, William Bendat and Lisa Raufman. *The Career Fitness Program: Exercising Your Options, Sixth Edition* Upper Saddle River, NJ: Pearson Custom Publishing, 2001.

Swinburne, Richard. *The Existence of God. 2nd Edition*. Oxford University Press, 2004.

The Holy Bible, *King James Version*. Nashville, TN: Crusade Publishers, Inc., 1977.

The New Interpreter's One Bible Volume Commentary on the Bible. Editorial Board, David L. Petersen, Beverly R. Gaventa, Nashville, TN: Abingdon Press, 2010.

Thomas, Terry, DMin. January 2013, Intensive Lecture, United Theological Seminary, Dayton, Ohio.

Tiffany, Frederick C. and Sharon H. Ringe, *Biblical Interpretation: A Road Map*. Nashville, TN: Abingdon Press, 1996.

Torbert, William. R. *The Practice of Action Inquiry*, in P. Reason and H. Bradbury (eds), *Handbook of Action Research: Participative Inquiry and Practice*. London: Sage, 2001.

Turner, Rev. Dr. Michael C. *The Miracle Center of Faith Missionary Baptist Church*. Capitol Heights, MD. MCFMBC Publishing, 1991.

Turabian Kate L. *A Manual for Writers of Term Papers, Theses, and Dissertations*. 7th Edition, Chicago, IL: The University of Chicago Press, 2007.

Varghese, Roy Abraham. *The Wonder of the World: A Journey from Modern Science to the Mind of God*. Fountain Hills, Arizona: Tyr Publishing. 2004.

Vyhmeister, Nancy Jean. *Quality Research Papers for Students of Religion and Theology*. Grand Rapids, MI: 2008.

Weems, Lovett Jr. *Church Leadership: Vision, Team, Culture, Integrity* Nashville, TN: Abingdon Press, 2010.

Welch, Adam C. *The Work of the Chronicler. Its Purpose and Its Date* London UK: Oxford University Press, 1939.

Williams, Thomas. *Augustine, On Free Choice of the Will*. Hackett Publishing Co., Indianapolis, IN, 1993.

Willimon, William H. Pastor: *The Theology and Practice of Ordained Ministry*. Nashville, TN. Abingdon Press, 2002.

Wilson C. and Herman H. Horne. *Jesus the Master Teacher*, Grand Rapids, MI: Baker Book House, 1974.

Wright, Nicholas. T. *The New Testament and the People of God: Christian Origins and the Question of God*. London, UK: SPCK, 1992.

Yin, Robert K. *Case Study Research: Design and Method*. Newbury Park, CA: Sage Publications Inc., 1989.

Zuck Roy. *Teaching As Jesus Taught.* Eugene, OR: Wipf and Stock Publishers, 2002

———. *Teaching with Spiritual Power*, Grand Rapids, MI: Kregel Pubns, 1963.

www.ingramcontent.com/pod-product-compliance
Lightning Source LLC
LaVergne TN
LVHW051501070426
835507LV00022B/2869